Creating a Culture
of Profitability

Creating a Culture of Profitability

A Revolutionary Model for Managing Culture

by Rob and Aviva Kleinbaum

Probabilistic Publishing

Editors: Dave and Debbie Charlesworth
Associate Editor: Nancy Winchester
Cover Concept: Sarah Golliher

Initial printing: October, 2013

Probabilistic Publishing   www.decisions-books.com
                                              e-mail: dave@decisions-books.com

Florida:
5715 NW 67th Ct
Gainesville, FL 32653
352-338-1789

Texas:
1702 Hodge Lake Ln
Sugar Land, TX 77478
281-277-4006

Written, designed, and printed in the United States of America.

Library of Congress Control Number: 2013956382

ISBN: 096479389–X
ISBN 13: 9780964793897
ISBN 13: 9781941075005 (digital editions)

To our three sons: Ian, Aric, and Danny, who taught us more than we are willing to admit.

Preface and Acknowledgments

First, a note on "voice." We go back and forth between the first person singular and plural. When we use singular voice, Rob is talking about his experiences (usually in a context that should make it obvious). We hope we have not caused any unnecessary confusion by switching back and forth between singular and plural pronouns. We have done our best to keep the tone light and informal. The subject is serious, but there is no reason the language has to be dull.

Thanks to Lawrence Harrison for bringing us into his work family and for creating the immense intellectual foundation on which the work rests, as well as his insightful and detailed comments on this work.

Three successful but different businessmen – David Jerome, Greg Powel, and Nick Pudar – offered wonderful advice. The participants at the Society of Decision Professionals 2013 Workshop, "Managing Alligators," were generous and thoughtful in their suggestions; they also reinforced our belief in the applicability of these ideas to managing projects.

The brilliant and eclectic participants of the Samuel Huntington Memorial Symposium: *Culture, Culture Change, and Economic Development* that took place in Moscow in 2010 provided a world class forum for discussing the main ideas in this book.

Our editors, Dave and Debbie Charlesworth, provided constant comments that shaped and focused the ideas, bringing their own long experience in business as well as their editing skills to bear on the work. Nancy Winchester offered helpful and gracious comments well beyond the call of duty.

Ian Mutchnick took time out of his crazy schedule as a neurosurgeon to make valuable comments about the neurological underpinnings of culture; this could well be the wave of the future. Dan Kleinbaum has been a deep contributor to this work for the last two years. It would not be here without his thoughtfulness, support, and effort. It is a great blessing to have worked together.

This book has been a joint labor of love between the two of us over the last five years directly and over the last 15 years working together, always trying to blend our different point of views. It helps to be in love with your co-author, especially when talking loudly through the disagreements. We are each here because of the other.

Publisher's Note

Two years ago Rob Kleinbaum and I talked at a Decision Analysis Affinity Group (DAAG) conference about a book he had started working on. Rob and his wife Aviva had studied fundamental sociological research that Lawrence Harrison and others had been doing on determining why some cultures succeed and others fail and were extending this thinking to a business context. This concept was intriguing, so we agreed to undertake the project. We went through many discussions and revisions of the text, especially as we got feedback from reviewers as noted in the Preface. In fact, it was just over a year ago when we provided our first comments back to Rob on the initial manuscript.

We believe the result is a powerful framework that gives managers and leaders the tools they need to create sustainable and profitable cultures within their organizations.

You might wonder why a publisher of decision analysis and game theory books would be interested in a book on business culture. The answer is simple: a company won't realize the full benefits of implementing decision analysis unless the culture is positive. The Kleinbaums have systematized, organized, and codified what most of us who work have intuited but never organized.

Another distinction relative to decision analysis (DA) is that DA can sometimes be implemented, at least partially, from the ground up (although a medium to high level sponsor is usually necessary). To change the culture, the top person within a unit or a team or a company *must* be either the instigator or at least integrally involved in and supportive of the effort.

We suggest that you first read the book for an overall view of the content. Then refer to Chapter 12, which discusses how to get started. An example from my background may be useful in illustrating some of the potential benefits of changing culture and providing direction on successful implementation.

I once worked as a technical team leader in a manufacturing plant. It was not a fun job – many of the negative cultural traits you're going to read about in this book were present. We probably had negatives relative to most of Rob's 13 aspects of cultural infrastructure (see Table 2.1).

In addition to manufacturing a large slate of products, our Division also had to interface with R&D and marketing. R&D would develop something to fill a marketing need, they'd sample the customer, and if the customer liked it, we'd have to scale it up. Many times there were significant problems with the scale up, which would anger marketing and R&D (they'd blame us and tell headquarters that were incompetent).

The Production Superintendent and the Division team leads (the Division Leadership Team), recognizing that we had an image problem relative the rest of the business, decided to try to improve our image. I had connectivity to an excellent Organizational Development "guru" named Ed Klinge, and Ed gave us a framework to use for us to work on the image problem. His framework was much more basic and "generic" than what the Kleinbaums present here, but it illustrates a successful approach.

We did a workshop, and started with the question, "What is our perception of our own image?" We filled several chart pad pages of comments, mostly negative. The next question was, "What do we do that contributes to this image?" Again, chart pad pages of stuff, 90% of it negative. This was very sobering. At the end of that exercise (the first phase of Workshop) everybody was really depressed, as we realized that we were our own collective worst enemy!

We condensed and reviewed our lists with the upper management on-site (no way we would have trusted the headquarters managers with any of this!), and they apologized, as they didn't realize that the climate was so bad. Then we collectively discussed the question, "Which of these items is the most important factor on our list?" There was a healthy debate, which we captured and we then agreed on the top one. The next question was, "What steps do we need to take to address this item?" This turned into a plan and time line on the whiteboard, which we all contributed to, agreed to do, and agreed to hold ourselves accountable for doing. We implemented the plan and the site upper management was right there with us supporting us. We completed the first item and then came back and did the second item on the list. After we did items 3 and 4, our performance, communication, and subsequently our reputation started to improve. We were slowly changing the culture.

These changes were subsequently put to the test. We had a new product that we failed several times to make in our equipment. The Production Superintendent had agreed to kill it. The marketing guy called and pleaded with me to intervene, as he had customers that loved the product samples they had obtained from R&D. We convened a workshop and used a very similar framework, but this time included R&D (which had heretofore been considered the enemy). It took 1/2 day just to ground everybody on the history of the product's R&D and the previous failed attempts. The workshop took two days. We ended up with a VERY detailed multi-color time line on the white-board wall of the conference room which everybody bought in to (even R&D and marketing) and they all had a role. Upon the "last chance" production run, we nailed it. One of the R&D team leaders spent a whole shift working at the front of the process helping an operator de-lump feed materials, which was unheard of. Even the most cynical operators were excited when the thing worked. We did a look-back workshop and agreed to work together (rather than blame each other) on subsequent new products. We changed the culture. It can be done!

The lessons learned relative to this book include:

1. *Top Down.* Culture change has to be top down, but in our case, a member of the Leadership Team (me) did catalyze it. I was fortunate to have a progressive and competent Division Superintendent – we would not have been successful without his active involvement, participation, and support.

2. *No Shotguns!* Don't take a "shotgun" approach to changing culture – pick out the top one or two items and address them thoroughly before moving on to the next items that you need to work on.

3. *Culture can be improved.* This book gives you a powerful tool kit to get started.

We would sincerely like to hear your comments relative to this book, especially successful examples. Please e-mail dave@decisions-books.com, and we sincerely wish you success in your endeavors.

Dave and Debbie Charlesworth
Probabilistic Publishing
October, 2013

Contents

1

Introduction: A Better Way

I knew that corporate culture carried much of the blame when, after 25 years of working either for or with General Motors (GM), I watched the company deteriorate and go bankrupt.

GM's response to the crisis in 2008 and early 2009 reflected its fundamental beliefs about the way the world works and was consistent with what it had been doing for the last 30 years: cut "structural costs," wait for future products to bring salvation, and count on cash from other regions to help prop things up. In the meantime, make no fundamental change in the business, its structure, or people running it (as they are clearly the best and brightest, know how to manage in a serious way, and have a sound plan). Proposed changes were touted as "profound" and "fundamental" but were really the minimum change from status quo the company believed it could get away with. GM leadership was unwilling to make necessary but painful long-term changes; instead there was continual compromise of action that only delayed disaster. This was reflected in every aspect of the enterprise, from decisions on manufacturing, which never brought capacity into line with market realities, to people, where almost no one was ever let go for poor performance.

GM's corporate culture had become unhealthy and self-destructive. Lack of customer awareness and the strong insular nature of its culture sent GM down a path towards bankruptcy well before the onset of the economic crisis. GM was so out of touch with the market they could not capitalize on innovations and changing customer needs, even though they had many of the technologies and ideas to do so. They failed to stay competitive.

I knew that culture was an important factor contributing to GM's failure and that there had to be an explanation and a solution to the problem of poor organizational culture. The best business writings on organizational culture – Argyis[1], Schein[2], and Kotter[3] – assign the success and failures of companies to their cultures but did not go far enough to be useful and none did a great job of describing what I was seeing. Because GM's culture was so destructive, I wondered if there were organizations with cultures that led them to be successful. There must be a better way!

The path to creating this book began with *Culture Matters*[4] by Lawrence Harrison and Samuel Huntington, two of the leading experts in economic development. These scholars addressed a fundamental question: *Does culture matter in societal development?* Harrison and Huntington made a compelling case: *culture matters a great deal.* They uncovered the specific traits that lead a society to progress or prevent it from doing so. Their work provided a rigorous way to think about culture that is based on evidence. They found that some cultures are able to create and foster consistent strong development, but some flounder despite huge amounts of international aid. Their explanation was brilliant. Surmising that these same cultural traits that Harrison and Huntington found to be important in a society would also apply to private enterprise, I took their model and applied it as a filter to analyze GM's culture. The product was a paper I wrote in March 2009, *Retooling GM's Culture* (see Appendix).

Retooling resonated with nearly every GM manager and professional below the management committee that was making the corporate decisions. It also resonated with many outsiders. The most compelling e-mails were from GM people who noted that the paper echoed their experience and wanted to know how they could help. The desire by members of the organization to belong to a healthy culture was so strong that it was almost heartbreaking. It showed the deeply human side of understanding culture – it matters to the lives of people. When *Retooling* circulated widely in government and industry, many

---

1 Argyris, Chris. (1993) *Knowledge for Action: A Guide to Overcoming Barriers to Organizational Change*, Jossey-Bass.
2 Schein, Edgar. (2010) *Organizational Culture and Leadership* 4th Edition, Jossey-Bass.
3 Kotter, John and James Hesket. (1992) *Corporate Culture and Performance*, Free Press.
4 Harrison, Lawrence and Samuel Huntington. (2001) *Culture Matters: How Values Shape Human Progress*, Basic Books.

industry experts, executives, consultants, and journalists said that the paper was the best description of the culture they had seen. Senior management, starting with the CEO, was furious; they immediately canceled my contract and said that I would never work at GM again (nor have I). So clearly I was on to something.

One unexpected result of *Retooling* was that Lawrence Harrison brought me into his professional family and invited me to join the executive committee of the Cultural Change Institute at Tufts University. He inspired me to work more deeply on the role of culture in business. This involved addressing the fundamental question that he had asked concerning nations:

> Is there a definition of "good" *corporate* culture – culture that leads to lasting business success?

This book answers the question and the answer is "Yes."

We have created a useful map where there was once only a vague sketch with many regions marked *terra incognito*. The map's value is the power it gives business leaders to navigate their way and manage culture to the same degree they can manage other important and complex drivers of profitability such as cost, customers, R&D, and so on. Managing culture will still need insight, diligence, creativity, and work, just as these other drivers do, but the map we provide is a big improvement over today's ad hoc treatment of culture. Like any map, its worth is how it gets you to your destination, not the detail on every space between here and there.[5]

1.1 What do we Mean by "Culture?"

Before laying out the details, we need to create two key building blocks: what we mean by "culture" and what makes a culture "good."

> *Culture* is the values, beliefs, attitudes, and assumptions shared within a company.

Culture includes all the shared mental baggage people carry with them. Behind any string of complicated logic lies the assumptions giving a thought shape. Culture is what defines those assumptions and, therefore, includes the reasoning and logic people use when they are making decisions. These beliefs and behaviors are brought to one decision after another, leading to success or failure. Culture affects the

---

5   Giere, Ronald (2006) *Scientific Perspectivism*, University of Chicago Press.

success of the company through the quality (or lack of quality) of the decisions that management makes.

Business culture helps people decide quickly by making the basic rules clear and aligning the company. People at all levels understand their role and what they are supposed to do without having to be told. The success of many companies, including Chevron, McKinsey, P&G, Honda, WL Gore, and Pixar is attributed to their cultures. A recent study of Toyota concluded that its success is due as much to its culture as to the Toyota Production System.[6]

Despite all this, mentioning the "C" word makes eyes roll, as it is seen as too "soft" to deal with operationally and does not matter anyway, once the "real stuff" has been taken care of. Business leaders know that culture is important but are frustrated with the lack of tools and specifics available to improve culture. Academic business theory is either too general or too daunting to be useful. Defining a good culture as adaptable and appropriate is hard to argue with but is not very helpful. A theory of culture needing an army of outsiders led by a genius professor to manage is not going to be "scalable," as we say today. Much of the research is driven by ideology and "positive" values from people with little understanding of business and only a vague notion that profits are important. Authors assert values that sound good, but do not have a convincing story on how culture adds to profits.

1.2 What is a "Good" Culture?

We define a "good" culture very simply:

A good culture is a culture that leads to a profitable, sustainable, healthy business.

Our focus is on sustaining a healthy and profitable business, not morals or aesthetics. Profitability is the outcome of success, that is, a measurement or indicator of how healthy your business is. If an idea does not contribute to the long-term health of a company, it should be tossed aside. We are not saying greed is good; it is not, for reasons we will discuss later. However, without profit, your business will be neither sustainable nor healthy. Robert Heinlein once said "Blessed are the rich in spirit, for they shall make dough."[7]

---

6   Takeuchi, Hirotaka, Emi Osono, and Norihiko Shimizu (2008) "The Contradictions that Drive Toyota's Success" Harvard Business Review.

7   Heinlein, Robert. (1961) *Stranger in a Strange Land*, Putnam.

Now that we've defined "good" culture, is there such a thing, and if so, what is it? The current consensus in literature is that the only universal characteristics of a good culture are adaptability and fit. This is not very useful. People need more depth to improve culture and business leaders are frustrated with the literature. It is like reducing marketing to "give customers what they want" or managing costs to "keep costs as low as possible."

An unsatisfactory answer does not always mean an incorrect answer. Our cure for the common cold is rest and chicken soup, and that is the extent of our understanding whether we like it or not. For culture, however, there is a much richer answer that we will develop.

People who care about the development of countries have looked at the role of culture for a long time, e.g. Weber's *The Protestant Ethic and the Spirit of Capitalism*, published in 1905. Over the last 20 years, there has been new research on the subject, initiated and led by Lawrence Harrison (mentioned earlier) and the Cultural Change Institute at Tufts. The Institute focused on how culture contributes to the prosperity and democracy of nations and published their findings in three major works: *Culture Matters* (2001), *The Central Liberal Truth* (2006), and *Jews, Confucians, and Protestants: Cultural Capital, and the End of Multiculturalism* (2012), with three volumes of supporting studies.

One of their important findings is that policy interventions need to consider culture, both in considering the causes of the problem and its cure. Naïve policy prescriptions that are oblivious to cultural issues are likely to fail. This also holds true for managing business problems. Culture is often a key part of many business challenges and needs to be part of the solution. Without this awareness, people will often work on the wrong issues.

Harrison and his colleagues (led by Mariano Grondona) found 25 attributes that define whether a culture is good[8], i.e. leads to economic success and democracy (see Appendix for a full listing). These attributes have been empirically validated[9] and are compelling. These are the values shared by the most successful societies on Earth and by the highest achieving minorities within them. Harrison calls them collectively a country's *cultural capital*. This is a powerful idea that applies to companies as well.

8   Harrison, Lawrence. (2013) *Jews, Confucians, and Protestants: Cultural Capital and the End of Multiculturalism*, Rowman and Littlefield.

9   They were independently tested in the World Values Survey. Ronald Inglehart, "Testing the Progress Typology," presented at the final Culture Matters Research Project conference at the Fletcher School, Tufts University, March 27-8, 2004, p. 10.

It is a short leap to assert that the same values that lead to prosperity for nations also lead to prosperity for companies, since a nation's wealth depends heavily upon the success of its businesses. These 25 attributes are the starting point for thinking about what defines a good culture for companies, but there are three reasons they must be modified:

♦ Some, such as child rearing, do not apply.

♦ A company is part of larger society and we know that the company's culture plays an important role in how well it fits into the surrounding society. For example, German and Japanese companies hold different cultural norms within their respective national cultures.

♦ Companies possess a core purpose beyond making money that defines the heart of their values. This purpose differs from company to company, even for close competitors in the same markets.

Leo Tolstoy famously said, "All happy families resemble one another; each unhappy family is unhappy in its own way." This quote sheds insight on understanding business culture and differences between companies. *All good cultures look alike, as they share many of the same characteristics.* Even in different places and industries, healthy companies all have a clear purpose, fit well within the larger society and markets, and live by a set of values that drive business success.

However, culture can go bad and drive failure in many ways, so there will be differences between the "unhappy" companies with a poor culture: some will be buggy makers in a world of automobiles, some have poor ethics, some are insular, some will be torn apart by internal silos, and so on.

1.3 How this Book is Organized

The next chapter defines a "profitable culture," presenting the main ideas and concepts. The will give you a clear understanding of the structure of a good culture.

The following chapters form the heart of the book: how to diagnose and manage culture. For each cultural value, we discuss:

- Forces leading to decay, which we refer to as the forces of entropy,
- Symptoms allowing diagnosis, and
- Remedies for restoring cultural health, both for upper management and for middle management.

In discussing how culture decays, we contrast what makes a company successful with what leads to decay. We liken cultural decay to entropy, that is, natural forces that lead to decay.

We discuss detailed symptoms on the health of each part of corporate culture. This permits a company to develop an early warning system and to understand specific cultural problems.

When presenting remedies, we distinguish between actions top management can take and those middle management can take. Both are important, but the respective span of control and roles are different, so separate tools are necessary. Both the top manager and middle manager should recognize what aspects of culture are within their span of control and have a conceptual model and set of tools to restore cultural health to their organization.

Following the chapters on diagnosis and treatment there is a chapter on managing the ways that culture preserves and protects itself. This issue cuts across different cultural traits and merit its own chapter.

We then discuss how a company should begin to implement culture management, including specific steps and tools. We suggest organizational roles and responsibilities for managing culture on an ongoing basis. Each company will need its own solution, but the initial road map can help it get started. We include a chapter on dealing with a strong but unhealthy culture.

The next chapter is titled "Managing Alligators." It focuses on how to survive cultural issues when running a project. The purpose is to give the tools for anticipating culture-related problems at the beginning of a project. This allows the team to plan for and manage them.

The final chapters include an empirical test of our key idea: right culture leads to profitability. While the results must be read with some caution, they are encouraging.

We are now ready to discuss a *culture of profitability*.

2
A Profitable Culture

The first step to fill in the sparse map of culture is to split corporate culture into four distinct parts, each with its own role:

- *Core purpose* – the guiding objective or principle that sets the organization's direction – its raison d'être.
- *Instrumental values* – links between the external environment and the firm.
- *Cultural infrastructure* – traits necessary for sustainable success for all companies, although their relative importance will vary. These traits drive good decisions throughout the enterprise.
- *Self-preserving mechanisms* – the ways in which culture becomes deeply embedded within the enterprise, ensuring compliance and punishing those who would change it; almost a living thing in its tenacity and will, not a set of ephemeral values.

This is a fundamental redrawing of the map of culture, replacing "Here be Dragons" with a map that supports navigation and management.

The following sections discuss these distinctive parts of culture and describe how they can contribute to making a culture "good" or healthy, ultimately leading to profitability.

2.1 Core Purpose

The first part of a company's culture is its *core purpose* or *reason for being*. This is the true heart of the enterprise – what people really want to do and where they want to go. To be useful, the purpose must be broadly understood and specific enough to guide action, otherwise it will not align people within the company. The core purpose is the "North Star" and ensures that the countless decisions summing up to success are pointed in the right direction. When the core purpose is clearly understood by all, senior leaders do not need to micromanage as lower levels understand the rules. Any employee should be able to tell, with a little reflection, if their action supports the company's purpose.

Healthy companies have a reason for being beyond making money; money is a means to an end, not the end in itself, as Peter Drucker pointed out long ago[1] and Jim Collins recently reasserted.[2] Whole Foods' purpose is to sell the highest quality organic and natural products. Wal-Mart's is "Save money. Live better." At GM under Alfred Sloan it was "A car for every purse and purpose." At Boeing the value was, before the 1990s, "To eat, breathe and sleep the world of aeronautics." At Pfizer it is "Life." DuPont's used to be "Better things for better living through Chemistry." As John F. Akers, a retired chairman of IBM and for many years a Times company board member, put it, "Making money so that you could continue to do good journalism was always a fundamental part of the thinking."[3] The company's founders often establish the purpose of the enterprise and then reinforce it over time. Sometimes it is accurately reflected in the mission statement but often is implicit.

There can be a wide range within any given industry. Honda's purpose ("Respect for the individual" and "The Three Joys of buying, selling and creating") and Toyota's ("Create a more prosperous society through automotive manufacturing") reflect real differences between the two companies, despite both being manufacturers with similar products in the same markets. Honda's frisky, upstart nature and Toyota's emphasis on manufacturing greatness accurately show their different purposes.

Greed is not good. The importance of steering action explains why greed is not profitable. Avarice provides little guidance on what to do. "Shareholder value" is a meaningless guide to action; does every listed stock have the same purpose? Given the same problem, shareholder value makes no distinction in how Toyota or Johnson and Johnson should act.

---

1   Drucker, Peter. (2006) *Classic Drucker: Essential Wisdom of Peter Drucker,* HBR Press.

2   Collins, Jim and Jerry Poras. (1990) *Built to Last,* Harper Business.

3   Quoted in New York Times obituary of Arthur Sulzberger, September 29, 2012.

There is a long track record of firms that decided to emphasize shareholder value and suffered as a result, from Boeing in the 1990's, to Citigroup, Northern Rock, Countrywide, Enron, and many others. Bausch and Lomb is a good example of a company that moved rather mindlessly outside its core area, losing shareholder value in the process, before retreating back to its fundamentals.[4]

As Jack Welch said, "The idea that shareholder value is a strategy is insane."[5] The person considered to be the world's greatest stock picker, Warren Buffet, has repeatedly denounced short-term thinking and greed as destructive of shareholder value.[6] There is a compelling body of evidence that there is no correlation between CEO pay and corporate performance.[7] The faulty assumptions in the intellectual underpinnings of shareholder value as a primary purpose have been compellingly shown.[8]

Instead of aligning an organization, greed tears it apart by fostering an ethos of everyone for himself. There is little cooperation for a common purpose, only utilitarian relationships based on reciprocal favors. Greed can motivate and energize people to a point – it *adds horsepower to your engine, but it should never be behind the steering wheel.*

2.2 Instrumental Values

The second part of a company's culture is *instrumental values,* which are traits that support its business, purpose, and environment. These traits control the *strategic* fit of the culture. Silicon Valley start-ups are informal in style because of the nature of the work and the

---

4   Zook, Chris. (2007) "Finding Your Next Core Business," Harvard Business Review.

5   Guerrera, Francesco. (2010) "Welch Condemns Share Price Focus," Financial Times http://www.ft.com/cms/s/0/294ff1f2-0f27-11de-ba10-0000779-fd2ac.html. Also Kay, John. "Greed isn't as good as we thought," Financial Times.

6   Buffet, Warren and Lawrence Cunningham. (2008) *The Essays of Warren Buffet: Lessons for Corporate America* 2nd Edition, Cunningham Group.

7   Fox, Justin and Lorsch, Jay. (2012) "What Good are Shareholders?" Harvard Business Review, citing Baruch Lev (2011), *Winning Investors Over*, Harvard Business Review Press.

8   Stout, Lynn. (2012) "The Problem of Corporate Purpose," Issues in Governance Studies, Brookings Institution http://www.brookings.edu/~/media/research/files/papers/2012/6/18%20corporate%20stout/stout_corporate%20issues.pdfresearch/files/papers/2012/6/18%20corporate%20stout/stout_corporate%20issues.pdf.

particular abilities of the people recruited. Old style bankers (not that there are any left) exuded probity and formality to win the trust of their depositors. Bond traders value the rough-and-tumble of aggressive play because these characteristics help them win. Firms with lifetime employment value "niceness" because the same people will likely be working with one another again, perhaps with reporting roles reversed. Issues such as national identity and individual taste come in play in this area of culture as well. There are differences between Americans, Japanese, and Germans that lead to differences in business cultures even in the same industry and markets.[9]

This part of culture has received the most attention but is, we think, the least important. When these traits go wrong, it is more of a nuisance than a calamity. Yes, sitting on a Japanese business card can cause pained expressions. Germans and French in the same meeting need strong facilitation to avoid unfortunate recurrences of history. And, you'd better not make jokes about religion if you are working south of the Mason-Dixon Line! But, problems in these areas are usually dealt with quickly and easily and seldom sources of either destruction or soaring success. Many solutions work: some investment banks succeed without being hyper aggressive, niceness is not always important in long term employment, and so on.

2.3 Cultural Infrastructure

The third part of culture is the *cultural infrastructure*. These are the core values all companies must have to be profitable. *One of this book's major contributions is the concept of a "cultural infrastructure."* Just as all societies need an infrastructure to function, all companies need a set of values to achieve sustained profitability. An important part of our argument is that these values are common across all companies. Every society needs roads, water, power, and sewers to work at a basic level, and a rule of law, an education system, a military, and so on, to develop. Different countries will use these to differing degrees, but all have them. Harrison's path-breaking discovery was that there are common traits to all successful societies; we believe the same is true for the prosperity of private enterprise as well.

These are the 13 key cultural values derived from the work of Harrison and his colleagues. These fall into four major categories. Just as all societies need an infrastructure, these values provide the cultural

---

9   Hofstede, Geert and Hofstede, Gert Jan. (2005) *Cultures and Organizations: Software of the Mind*, McGraw Hill.

infrastructure enabling consistently profitable decisions. These cultural values are summarized in Table 2.1 below.

Cultural Infrastructure		
External Focus	1.	**External Focus.** People identify broadly with groups beyond the company and into society.
Internal Trust	2.	**Internal Trust.** Trust and cooperation across internal boundaries are valued.
The Role and Qualifications of Leadership	3.	**Merit and Accountability.** Enterprise holds leaders accountable and merit is central to advancement.
	4.	**Debate, Dissent, and Discipline.** Leadership is offered respect, but is never worshipped. In turn, debate and dissent are encouraged, accompanied by discipline in execution.
	5.	**Empowered.** People believe they can influence their destiny.
	6.	**Decisions Where They Belong.** Authority is decentralized and horizontal.
Time Orientation	7.	**Forward Looking.** People emphasize the future, not the past.
	8.	**Frugality and Investment.** Frugality and investment are both valued.
	9.	**Innovation.** Innovation is valued
Basics	10.	**Strong Work Ethic.** Work is central in healthy companies.
	11.	**Ethics.** Ethical codes are important.
	12.	**Continuous Learning.** Ongoing education is important.
	13.	**Ability Matters Most.** Ability is valued, regardless of gender, pedigree, religion, or race.

Table 2.1: Values of a Profitable Cultural Infrastructure

There are several reasons to feel confident accepting these principles:

♦ There is a compelling logic to them.
♦ Data strongly support them.
♦ They make sense for an enterprise for the same reasons they make sense for a nation.
♦ They are easy to understand.
♦ They contain enough detail to be useful.
♦ They can be tested against experience and data.

We can think of companies whose values were not aligned with these that did well in the short run, but in the long run developed deep problems and in some cases have gone out of business. There is not a single business currently regarded as a benchmark company that violates these cultural norms.

We will now discuss each trait of the cultural infrastructure in more detail.

External Focus

1. **External focus**. To be successful, a company must see the world as it is. Customers, government, technology, and competitors are basic forces that either create success or drive a company into bankruptcy.

People identify broadly with groups beyond the company and into society at large. When people in a company identify with outsiders, they develop the right products. The enterprise has an inborn understanding of its customers and an authentic wish to serve them well. A business that views its customers as "people like us" places importance on producing shared value and gains the trust of its customers.

> When a blizzard struck the Midwest a few years ago, Southwest kept the planes at the gate even though it meant a black mark in "on time" measurements. The gate agents and flight attendants, without any orders from management, ordered pizza and gave a party. Understanding their customer, plus empowerment (which we will discuss shortly), let Southwest turn the event into a positive experience for their customers.

> Northwest planes, however, were stuck on the runways for a long time, enraging passengers. They finally returned to the gates, but only because the CEO happened to be stuck on the tarmac

himself and demanded in a fury to bring the planes in. Northwest later went bankrupt and was purchased by Delta; Northwest no longer exists.

An outward-looking company understands and manages the needs of other parties critical to success, such as governments, civil society, suppliers, and allies. Alliances become workable, relations with regulators become productive, and civil society is engaged, not hostile. GE has done a marvelous job at engaging with civil society and government and is one of the most respected companies in the world. GM, a deeply insular company, never managed any of its alliances well and received little benefit from them. GM's products did not consistently meet the needs of the parts of society it found the most alien: upscale consumers who liked high quality, fuel-efficient vehicles.

If an enterprise is in touch with the broader world, its managers see what is coming and adapt. They are attuned to important trends in society and understand their implications for business. Their sensitive radar picks up changes in tastes, new technologies, evolving public policy or novel competitors. They are driven to innovation and commercial success, not roiled by change. Toyota built hybrids far earlier than its more insular competitors. In contrast, IBM did not understand the implications of turning over the PC operating system business to Microsoft.

Internal Trust

2. **Internal Trust**. Internal trust enables people to "work together for a common purpose."[10] An external focus helps a business know what to do; internal trust enables them to do it.

Internal trust helps information flow within the enterprise and this is the life-blood of good decision making. Groups and teams share intelligence, treating knowledge as a weapon against their competitors, not against each other. Effective decision making becomes easier because of timely and accurate information. Each group does its best to make sure integration takes place across the functions and business units. Modern business is a constant dance with multiple and shifting internal partners who must act in step; it only works when people trust one another to do their part.

In large companies trust must be built on more than personal relationships, because people cannot know one another well. This is

---

10 Fukuyama, Francis. (1996) *Trust: The Social Virtues and the Creation of Prosperity*, Free Press.

why trust in fellow workers becomes such an important value; little will happen without it. Disney redefined its business as share of "entertainment wallet" by connecting its theme parks, hotels, and movie divisions. On the other hand, a recent article on Microsoft discussed how many good ideas within the company failed to reach implementation because its internal parts worked so poorly together.[11]

The Role and Qualifications of Leadership

The darker nature of leadership is that some people want power for its seductive headiness and others want to surrender it to avoid responsibility.[12] This is a great deal easier than empowering others, taking responsibility, and holding yourself and others accountable. But that *is* the role of leadership.

3. **Accountability and Merit**. A healthy enterprise holds leaders accountable and merit is central to advancement. Leaders perform well and, if not, they are replaced by people who do. The result is stronger leadership. The importance of accountability has been stated many times but the clearest was given by Drucker in 1967:[13]

> "It is the duty of the executive to remove ruthlessly anyone—and especially any manager—who consistently fails to perform with high distinction. To let such a man stay on corrupts the others. It is grossly unfair to the whole organization. It is grossly unfair to his subordinates who are deprived by their superior's inadequacy of opportunities for achievement and recognition. Above all, it is senseless cruelty to the man himself. He knows that he is inadequate whether he admits it to himself or not."

If leaders are neither chosen on merit nor held accountable, then they are picked on the basis of patronage, reciprocal favors, or membership in some group having little to do with performance. Mediocrity stays in place and profits decline unless the company is shielded from market forces. We will say more about leadership later, but for now this captures the core of what we think is important about choosing and keeping leaders. In a recent and wonderful essay, Thomas Ricks discussed how several factors in the 1950's let the US Army to lose

---

11 Brass, Dick. (2010) "Microsoft's Creative Destruction," New York Times.
12 Fromm, Eric. (1965) *Escape from Freedom*, Holt. Originally published in 1941 to explain the rise of authoritarian political regimes.
13 Drucker, Peter (1967) *The Effective Executive*, Harper and Row.

the value of accountability.[14] This led to an officer corps in Vietnam where "honesty and accountability were replaced by deceit and command indiscipline." The results were disastrous.

4. **Debate, Dissent, and Discipline.** Good leaders are vigilant and encourage broad engagement from their people. This trait enhances a company's ability to make complex decisions. In a changing environment, business needs a constant retesting of assumptions. Dissent lets the organization hear signals of change clearly and correct itself after making errors. Debate makes the company smarter and produces better solutions. This must be accompanied by discipline after a decision is made, but people on the front lines must be expected to point out when a plan is not working and corrections are required. Allowing debate and dissent gives people control over their destiny and empowers them to act; this draws more workers into taking responsibility for the enterprise and acting as leaders.

This is seen as one of the main reasons Israel has been so successful in creating startups. This trait is deeply embedded into the national culture.[15] It avoids the danger of becoming "lemmings" – a few leaders marching boldly where they have no business going and followers going along to their end (as Alfred, Lord Tennyson put it, "Into the valley of death rode the six hundred...").

Effective dissent and debate are not possible in a culture where leaders are worshipped. No one wants to argue with a god and gods do not want to be argued with.

5. **Empowered.** When people believe they can influence their own destiny, they act accordingly. Individually and collectively they show leadership in creating a future. Much has been written about empowerment, but it is simply people believing they hold the right and ability to act, and is important to a healthy enterprise. As Jack Welch put it, "You've got to reach to every level of your organization and find every place where knowledge may live ... Leadership is not about dictating, it's about empowering employees so that they recognize their ability to take action."[16]

---

14 Ricks, Thomas (2012), "Whatever Happened to Accountability?" Harvard Business Review.

15 Senor, Dan and Singer, Saul (2011) *Start up Nation: The Story of Israel's Economic Miracle*, Twelve.

16 Welch, Jack (2006), Keynote To Franklin Covey Symposium, downloaded from http://www.leadershipnow.com/leadingblog/leadership.

6. **Decisions Where They Belong**. The people who understand the issues are the ones who should make the decisions. When executives near the issues make a choice, they are much more likely to use complete information and see important nuances. One of the more amusing examples of what happens when this is not done is when GM's headquarters in Detroit named a car, destined for Latin America, "Nova," which translates into Spanish as "No Go."

Another problem with centralized decision making is that the people in charge have too much on their plate. A large number of complex issues are funneled to the center, one after another, and have to be managed by the same few people. The result is that leaders cannot dedicate the time necessary to make good decisions as they do not understand the complexity, local factors, and the realities of implementation. A bias to action is wonderful but it must be wedded to the ability to make good decisions.

Time Orientation

A good definition of an adult is someone who balances yesterday, today, and tomorrow. Children only live in the moment; the senescent only live in the past. Success in the business world requires adults: people who understand the lessons and limitations of the past, manage the problems of today, and create the conditions for their future.

One aspect of proper time orientation is the willingness to seek serious solutions to serious problems, that is, to manage the immediate crisis *and* to do enough to solve the underlying problem. There is clear thinking about the future and how current actions will affect it. Most problems grow when untreated, so deferring pain means even stronger medicine is needed in the future.

Mature adults can tell when it is best to let things be. Time orientation strongly affects some of the fundamentals of economic success: control of costs, intelligent investments, and innovation. Companies with steady profitability are forward looking, set realistic goals, control their costs, and make sensible decisions about investments.[17]

7. **Forward Looking**. A healthy company should have more dreams than memories.[18] People emphasize the future, not the past. Do employees believe progress is realistic and attainable? Are they encouraged to plan and do they see the point of saving? In forward-looking

---

17 Buffet, Warren, op. cit.
18 I believe the origin of this wonderful phrase is Tom Friedman's *The Earth is Flat*, 2005. The application to corporate culture is mine.

companies, people understand how the past shaped the present and how the present creates their future. There is a Chinese proverb: If you are planning for a year, sow rice; if you are planning for a decade, plant trees; if you are planning for a lifetime, educate people.

8. **Frugality and Investment**. A belief in thrift and investing in the future helps a healthy company strike the right degree of sacrificing today for benefits tomorrow. A few years ago Carlos Ghosn, CEO of Renault-Nissan, coined the phrase "frugal engineering." The idea is to innovate intelligently and effectively under cost constraints.[19] Recent research has shown the importance of frugality to success and the large difference between frugality and cost control.[20] Here are two great quotes:[21]

> "How did we stay profitable..? I've always said – I think people are getting bored of hearing it – manage in good times so that you're ready for bad times... *We've always made sure that we never overreached ourselves. We never got dangerously in debt and never let costs get out of hand. And that gave us a real edge...*"– Herb Kelleher, CEO Southwest Airlines (emphasis added)

> "The true IKEA spirit is founded on our enthusiasm, on our constant will to renew, on our cost consciousness, on our willingness to assume responsibility and to help, on our humbleness before the task, and on the simplicity in our behavior...*waste of resources is a mortal sin at IKEA. Expensive solutions are often signs of mediocrity, and an idea without a price tag is never acceptable.*" – Ingvar Kamprad, founder of IKEA (emphasis added)

Consider the marketing extravaganzas of the dot.com boom: where all frugality was lost, investments made no sense, and costs ran wild. Many of these companies were clear examples of poor future orientation and did not stay in business.

9. **Innovation**. Valuing innovation is a condition for change. Companies will try new solutions instead of always repeating the "tried and true." Innovation drives technological improvements in products

---

19 Radjou, Navi, Jaideep Prabhu, and Simone Ahuja. (2012) "The CEO's Frugal Innovation Agenda," HBR Blog, http://blogs.hbr.org/cs/2012/10/the_ceos_frugal_innovation_age.html.

20 Anderson, Sheldon and Anne Lillis. (2011) "Corporate Frugality: Theory, Measurement, and Practice," Journal of Accounting Research. Downloaded from http://papers.ssrn.com/sol3/papers.cfm?abstract_id=1742115.

21 Anderson ibid.

and services and allows people to shift from old practices that are no longer competitive to new ones that are competitive. There is extensive literature on innovation, but little talk about it as a key cultural value. It is difficult to make the right level of investment and to make investment decisions among various opportunities. If managers believe innovation is necessary, the right logic and assumptions will channel the debate.

The Basics

The basics are, well, basic! Work, ethics, learning, and lack of misogyny and bigotry are fundamental values necessary for lasting success simply because their absence will lead to going out of business or being taken over. In many industries, these are taken for granted, but events keep showing that the basics are still an issue. We often hear of people we thought were trustworthy who are in fact criminal (for example, Bernard Madoff). Greed and ignorance still result in workplace accidents that injure and kill workers and others unnecessarily. The Macondo blow out demonstrated this and, with greater loss of life but less attention, so did recent factory fires in Pakistan and Bangladesh that killed 400 people. The fertilizer plant in West, Texas did not have a credible emergency management plan, which led to unnecessary emergency responder fatalities (the emergency responders had neither the training nor the equipment to fight an ammonium nitrate fire and should have been instructed to evacuate people from the vicinity in the event of a major fire). Lesser examples can be found every week in the headlines (as we write this, a headline in the Wall Street Journal is "UBS Faces $1 Billion Libor Fine").

10. **Strong Work Ethic**. No company will succeed without a belief in hard work. A "mañana" business culture is unlikely to survive much beyond tomorrow (unless protected by government).

A belief in hard work is what distinguishes the most successful subgroups of many countries. The success of Asians, Jews, West Indians, among many others, is partly attributable to their deep work ethic. It is an assertion on my part, but I am willing to state that behind every successful company is an ethic of hard work and doing whatever it takes to be successful. This is true of the small, high tech startups in Silicon Valley, where limitless hours are expected, to the Chaldean-owned produce stores here in Michigan, to the work-crazed entry-level Wall Streeters.

11. **Ethics**. Ethical codes provide the foundation for relationships with customers, other companies, and government. The public wants to buy goods from companies they trust; ethics matter. Ethical companies insist on a high degree of ethics in their partners and allies. They know that relationships need a foundation of trust and integrity; contracts are not enough. Government support is often necessary to operate and it will not be forthcoming to the tainted.

The boundaries of ethics now include a company's entire value chain. Many companies have been hurt more by businesses in their value chain than by their own actions. Coca-Cola was wounded by the actions of one of its bottlers (an independent company) in Latin America was accused of violently repressing unions. Nike was attacked for its use of sweat shops, all separate contractors. Home Depot was accused of deforesting large pieces of land through its purchasing policies. These events blindsided the companies – they neither anticipated nor managed them well, at least initially. As a result, they are now insisting on ethical behaviors in their suppliers and distributors as well as their own employees.

Corrupt companies seldom progress into lasting prosperity. Bankruptcy and in some cases prison for dishonest executives are likely results of poor ethics. Enron no longer exists and neither does Anderson.

12. **Continuous Learning**. Ongoing education is important to a healthy business. Valuing education is necessary because the modern business climate includes constant change in technology, markets, regulatory conditions, and customer tastes. GE's Crottonville is a premier in-house business school because it teaches how to manage change, not because of skills training. Education promotes an external perspective, innovation, intelligent dissent, skills, and employee loyalty – all valuable traits in business. A commitment to education also shows a commitment to tomorrow and winning the future.

13. **Ability Matters Most**. Companies that value ability *regardless of race, religion, pedigree, or gender* are harvesting all the talent they can. Capturing the contributions of large parts of the population means getting good ideas and winning the battle for talent. MIT has a better economics department than Harvard because Harvard chose exactly the wrong time to be anti-Semitic (right after WW II) and refused tenure to two future Nobel Prize winners.

Recent research shows that diversity of information and perspectives correlates with financial performance[22, 23] and team performance.[24] By its nature, a diverse company will understand these segments and be able to market to them. The public will often admire such companies, at least in the Western world, and attract "earned media" and favor from civil society. Governments will favor these businesses through the regulatory process, as many of their citizens are women and minorities.

2.4 Culture's Self-Preserving Mechanisms

Its core purpose, instrumental values, and cultural infrastructure are the defining values of a company and together form its culture. Managing culture cannot be done without understanding how these values are implanted and preserved within a company, which brings us to the fourth part of culture, self-preserving mechanisms.

Culture is much more than a set of disembodied values. It becomes entrenched into an organization, in its people, processes, and structures. Self-preserving mechanisms are the ways in which culture becomes deeply embedded within an enterprise such that change is very difficult.

There is an important distinction between a culture's health and its strength. Cultural health refers to how good or bad it is, whereas strength refers to how deeply embedded it is. Self-preserving mechanisms have to do with strength, not health. Many times we have seen companies with bad cultures that were very strong, GM being a case in point. Companies with bad and strong cultures descend into oblivion, although it can take a while for ruin to overtake them. We talk about how to manage this later.

---

22 Feng, Li and Venky Nagar. (2013) "Diversity and Performance," Management Science.

23 Credit Suisse, 2012, "Gender Diversity and Corporate Performance," August 2012 https://infocus.credit-suisse.com/data/_product_documents/_shop/360145/csri_gender_diversity_and_corporate_performance.pdf.

24 Bär, Michaela, Alexandra Niessen, Stefan Ruenzi. (2007) "The Impact of Work Group Diversity on Performance: Large Sample Evidence from the Mutual Fund Industry," CFR-Working Paper NO. 07-16. Also Hansen, Zeynep, Hideo Owan, and Jie Pan. (2006) "The Impact of Group Diversity on Performance and Knowledge Spillover – An Experiment in a College Classroom," NBER Working Paper.

Culture "Scales"

Culture becomes stronger with the size of the enterprise. There is a powerful "bandwagon" effect – the more people around you board the same bus, the harder it is for you to stay off it. As human beings, we find it difficult to march to a different drummer, especially in business. Daily interactions and informal feedback throw a web around people. The strength of the web is proportional to the number of interpersonal connections, which increase with the *square* of the number of employees. A culture shared by 1000 people is 100 times stronger than one shared by 100 people. The strength of the culture becomes formidable, as does the force on an individual's behavior.

Culture Becomes Encoded

In addition to the scale effect, culture can become encoded into formal processes and procedures. In small and young companies, the founding leadership drives the culture, mostly through informal means, and can easily change it. As companies grow, however, cultural values become written rules and informal but real constraints, especially in compensation, hiring and promotion, decision making, and budgeting. They shape decision rights and decision style. These strengthen the culture and subsequent adjustment becomes difficult. Over time, new ways become old ways, "how things are done," and part of the "normal" practices of business life.

Long-lived constraints become untested fences;[25] the belief about how business is done. For example, if a capital allocation decision needs a 50-page business plan, no projects without one will enter the system; people will not even try. If decision making needs a consensus, then no one will bother introducing something without universal appeal or without a long political campaign to make sure everyone is on board. A more subtle example: PowerPoint has embedded itself into many companies. It is taken for granted as the way information *should be* communicated. But PowerPoint can hinder two-way exchange and healthy debate. This obstructs information flow within the enterprise, reinforces hierarchy, stifles debate and dissent, and can even contribute to disaster.[26] People assume this is "normal" and are unlikely to see the cultural problem.

---

25 Skinner, B.F. (2005) *Walden Two*, Hackett. Originally published in 1976 by Macmillan.

26 Tufte, Edward. (2006) *The Cognitive Style of PowerPoint: Pitching Out Corrupts Within*, 2d Ed. Graphics Press. Tufte pointed out how PowerPoint contributed to the Challenger disaster.

Vested Interests

When a company creates a procedure, it creates a group of people responsible for managing and enforcing the procedure: "process cops." Now there is a group vested in the status quo.

Leaders who "come up through the system" will resist creating leaders who have not, as they want to make sure their replacements share their values and experiences. McKinsey is famous for this; so was IBM at one point. The Japanese car companies practice this, and so do their US counterparts.

People's emotions serve to preserve culture. Culture becomes ingrained in people at an emotional level. If someone proposes an action in alignment with these beliefs, people experience a feeling of harmony and pleasure. The opposite is just as true: when a proposal goes against the culture of the enterprise, it elicits fear and anger. People will strike at what they see as a threat to the business. The presence of these strong emotions, both joy and fear, make rational discussion difficult. This is especially important in older companies practicing lifetime employment. The company's cultural norms become the personal values of the employees.

Hard to Change

Culture becomes hard to change as it is implanted in the people, the work, and the formal procedures. There are many ways culture implants itself in a company, but the result is constraining the allowed choices: approval of new products, the hiring and promotion of people, use of information, and so on. A company with a healthy culture that supports its business can become a dynamo while a company with a bad but strong culture is headed for the bankruptcy courts or will be taken over.

In a strong culture, cultural change will be slow and difficult; rapid changes in values will be impossible. This is why some companies use "skunk works" to develop new ideas and why the skunk works culture rarely influences the larger organization: a small new group is fighting a larger, stronger, established set of values.

Consider the cultural strength of four organizations we are familiar with: "Old GM," a hospital, a shipping company, and a hotel company.

Four Example Cultures	Unhealthy	Healthy
Strong Culture	General Motors	Hospital
Weak Culture	Shipping Company	Hotel Company

Both the hospital and "Old GM" possess strong cultures – picture an intact castle with a moat. Anyone familiar with GM knows how strong its culture was; here is a good example of how strength and health do not always go hand in hand, at least in the short run.

Most people familiar with large hospitals would agree they have powerful cultures; changing anything is difficult. In this case the hospital is one of the nation's finest, with consistent top scores from rating agencies. Therefore, this is an example of a strong and healthy culture.

The other two examples are a shipping company and a hotel company, both of whose cultures were not deeply embedded enough to resist change. The shipping company's culture was in disarray because of some key changes made in the composition of its fleet. The company had combined officers from Europe, the US, and Asia, replaced the enlisted crews with Indians, and were in the midst of changing its officer fleet from European and American to Filipino. These changes were made to cut costs. While the company preserved a strong safety record, its culture was uprooted by these changes. All the unwritten rules were displaced and the transition led to disruptive tension. Internal trust was compromised, to say the least. The company had not anticipated these effects and failed to manage them well. There were serious consequences: labor turnover was much higher than expected and, according to several sources, operating effectiveness was hampered.

In the hotel example, an old company was taken over by new management who believed in the importance of culture and deliberately created a new one, beginning with establishing a clear purpose and moving on to leadership and internal trust. It was a young and healthy company in the process of being built with a coherent plan.

2.5 Adaptability

Along with strategic fit, adaptability is the only cultural trait recognized in the current business literature as universally good. In the model of culture we present here, adaptability is determined by five cultural values: the company's reason for being and four of the cultural infrastructure traits:

1. The enterprise's core purpose serves as a rudder to set the new direction.
2. An external perspective allows a business to see the need to adapt and avoid being blindsided.
3. Internal trust lets the parts of the enterprise act effectively.
4. The belief people can affect their destiny empowers them to act, to do what is required to create the world they want, to act with purpose and courage. This only happens when people think they can actually do something. When they don't, they become passive victims and sit there while "their iceberg melts."[27]
5. Valuing innovation encourages people to try new things in new ways rather than sticking to what they have done in the past.

The conclusion: adaptability is a natural result of a healthy core culture, and the definitions presented here help us understand it in greater depth.

2.6 Cultural Map Summary

Now that we have gone through the four parts of culture in detail, let us summarize by using a metaphor of taking a trip. The core purpose of the enterprise is its direction, the instrumental values are the vehicle it is using, and the infrastructure is the road.

This also helps explain their relative importance. If you are going in the wrong direction, you will not arrive at the desired destination, even if you have the right vehicle and good roads. But many different kinds of vehicles will do for most journeys, whether a Mini or a large utility vehicle. Your comfort and speed might be affected, but you will still get there. Without roads, you cannot travel anywhere, even with the greatest car in the world and a wonderful destination. Roads, however, only offer opportunity; much else is required to get to the destination. The cultural infrastructure is a necessary condition for profitability, but is not sufficient.

---

27 Kotter, John and Holger Rathgeber. (2005) *Our Iceberg is Melting*, St. Martins.

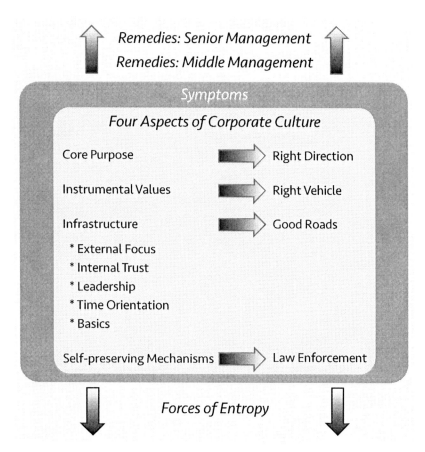

Figure 2.1: Cultural Map

Culture's self-preserving mechanisms serve as law enforcement or, perhaps, as a prison for imagination. This is how culture is enforced. Violators are punished and, by doing so, keep everyone else in line. The enforcement of laws has little to do with a law's merit. Bad laws can be as rigorously enforced as good ones. Corporate culture can take on a life of its own that is powerful and self-preserving. Cultural imperatives, though, are not laws of physics.

Companies can and must shape their culture. To do so, they need:

♦ A clear conceptual model of culture,

♦ Understanding of forces that lead to cultural decay (forces of entropy),

♦ Understanding of the symptoms that permit diagnosis of specific cultural ills, and

♦ Remedies (what senior and middle management can do about it).

This summarized in Figure 2.1, which serves as a road map for the book. We now turn discussing these ideas in greater detail.

3
Managing Culture – Overview

In the last section, we took the mystery out of culture. Culture is like any other important business driver: challenging but neither brain surgery nor mysticism.

The number one requirement for managing culture is the decision to do so. Every company creates its own way of managing important issues, with tracking, defined accountability, and an overall commitment to manage effectively. Once a company decides to treat culture like any other serious operating issue, half the battle is won. Our hope is the ideas we present here take away the mystery of managing culture. Once leadership understands that culture is no more puzzling than fixed costs or monthly sales, they can start to manage culture with the same vigor.

As noted in Section 1.3, we present four building blocks of effective management of culture:

1. Forces of entropy
2. Symptoms
3. Remedies – Senior Management
4. Remedies – Middle Management

These four items represent the road map for managing culture, and we will map these building blocks against each of the cultural values beginning with core purpose.

Managers need to understand the *forces of entropy* that shape culture and how these are tied to the growth and long term success of the company. People must understand how these seeds grow and the fruit they bear.

Given the nature of culture, leadership needs to recognize *symptoms* of cultural health and be able to distinguish good culture from bad culture. Culture can decay slowly as poor decisions are made or the wrong people are put in leadership. Understanding the symptoms permits management to spot problem areas and intervene before it is too late. We consider "healthy" and "unhealthy" aspects of each symptom. Life, of course, is a continuum and most companies will be somewhere in the middle. But taken together, these diagnostics give a clear and compelling picture of the state of a company's culture.

In discussing *remedies*, we will take the perspectives of top management and the working level manager. Both have important parts to play in keeping culture healthy, but their roles and perspectives differ in emphasis. Top management must have an accurate gauge on cultural health, be able to identify problems, be a force for change, provide support for actions that cross boundaries, and drive accountability. As culture cuts across the organization and values are driven from the top, senior leadership must ensure managers can work effectively.

The management team must do its part, but that is not enough to keep culture healthy or fix its problems. Working level managers own a critical role. They are the ones responsible for the many decisions controlling the health of the company and they are usually the first to notice problems.

Working level executives and managers are responsible for spotting problems, diagnosing them, and creating and carrying out solutions. Managers must be able to identify and solve problems as part of their normal work, without having to always go to the executive committee for support or permission. This will ensure that problems are caught early and managed at an early stage. Managers need a set of tools for managing culture. Like most issues, catching a cultural problem early makes a cure more likely to succeed and much less painful. The good news is that managers are capable of creating a healthy culture, as long as they have a conceptual framework, tools and guidance on what to do, and support from the top.

Managers have a dilemma: either confront the cultural problem impeding their objectives, or work around the problems, completing their individual missions but leaving the underlying problem to fester. In an ideal world, managers should always seek to fix the underlying problem. But life is not always that simple – sometimes discretion is the better part of valor and both the manager and organization are better off if the immediate problems are solved, even if the cultural problems are not addressed. We will offer both types of solutions to middle managers as we discuss how they can improve the culture of the company and get their work done despite cultural obstacles. There is a proverb that says it is hard to walk on two roads – our preference is for people at all levels to work on the underlying problem, but this will not always be possible. Even when compromise is necessary, middle managers must find a way to circle back to deal with the deeper problem. Otherwise the same problem will come back to haunt the manager and others.

3.1 General Symptoms

Before turning to specific cultural values, it is worth going over some general signs of cultural problems. These are symptoms of an untreated malaise and warnings of a deeper problem. They are summarized in Table 3.1.

Problem Solving

In healthy companies, solved problems stay solved. Sometimes issues will return as life is always developing new challenges, but there is a sense that problems are surfaced and dealt with.

In unhealthy companies, problems become hardy perennials and "Whack-A-Moles."

"Hardy perennials" are difficulties that keep recurring despite the belief they are solved. Like dandelions whose roots are alive, these issues come back again and again despite one "fix" after another. "Whack-a-moles" are the hardy perennials' first cousin. This is when a problem fixed in one place keeps cropping up in another place. These are clear signs of untreated systemic issues. Culture may or may not be the problem (there are other system-wide issues that can plague business), but these symptoms should ring alarm bells and trigger a different look at possible causes. Otherwise you become one of Einstein's bumblers – someone who does the same thing again and again and expects different results.

Track Record

Successful companies with good cultures have a record of success. Setbacks occur, but the overall trend is positive and profits are dependable, given the uncertainties of the market place and economy.

Issue	Unhealthy	Healthy
Problem Solving	Hardy perennials and Whack-a-moles	Solved problems stay solved
Track Record	Continual failure and ongoing optimism	Mostly success, setbacks faced and managed
Attitude Toward Culture	Jokes about the culture	Culture is not funny
Sensibility	People accept the absurd and futile as normal (signals terminal stage)	Sensible understanding of world; absurd is rejected out of hand

Table 3.1: General Symptoms of Cultural Problems

Companies with poor culture will have continual failure combined with unmerited optimism that the future will improve. When people repeatedly miss objectives and optimism constantly triumphs over experience, something is wrong. Smart people repeat failed actions again and again, yet continue to think everything is moving in the right direction. A common story often accompanies this behavior with the following three plot elements:

♦ Management is smart (they often are)
♦ They are doing well (they are not)
♦ But it will take time for plans to come to fruition and the next product will make it all right (it will not).

This sequence of reinforcing beliefs is hard to contradict, so it can persist for a long time, even to bankruptcy. This symptom is often glaringly obvious to outsiders but invisible to insiders. Unfortunately, this is the story that failed management uses to cling to their positions and delusions.[1]

Attitude Toward Culture

In companies with healthy cultures, you never hear anyone joke about it (unless they are looking at a Dilbert cartoon). There is simply nothing to laugh about.

A clear symptom of a bad culture is that it becomes a subject for jokes. The more severe the problem, the more prevalent the joking. Humor is a way to acceptably express the unacceptable, where the

---

1 James, David N. (2002) "The Trouble I Have Seen," Harvard Business Review.

surface and the truth are not in alignment.[2] People defuse important unresolved issues by minimizing their seriousness. Everything becomes a joke. Since jokes about culture cannot be interpreted as anything else, they are a sure sign something is amiss. People never joke about what is going well.

Sensibility

Well-run companies with good cultures have a general climate of sensibility. Leadership and staff seem sane and in touch with the world, with a realistic view of the world and themselves.

In very poor cultures, people accept the absurd and futile as normal. This symptom is the most disturbing. This is a glaring signal of a culture decayed beyond the point of repair.[3] For many years, this was a characteristic of GM, and, in conversations with people from other companies with similar issues, we have heard the same reports.

These are general alarm bells. None are decisive and they do not point to where the specific problem lies. We now turn to diagnosis and management of the specific parts of culture, beginning with the core purpose.

---

2   Lyttle, Jim. (2007)."Judicious Use and Management of Humor in the Workplace," Business Horizons.

3   Barzun, Jacques. (2001) *From Dawn to Decadence: 1500 to the Present: 500 years of Cultural Life*, Perennial.

4

Diagnosis and Treatment: Core Purpose

The core purpose of a company is, in many ways, the most important part of its culture. The purpose guides many decisions, including product development. It aligns the entire enterprise and lets everyone know why they are at work and, at a high level, what they should be doing. Just as important, it helps employees know what *not* to do. The core purpose is seldom managed, monitored, or maintained. Yet when the core purpose loses its effectiveness, this can significantly disrupt the company.

4.1 Forces of Entropy

The reason-for-being can degrade in four ways:

- Fundamental changes lead to irrelevance: you are a buggy maker in a world of automobiles,
- Loss of founder, who is replaced by professional managers who may lack passion and commitment,
- New recruits who are attracted by financial incentives rather than commitment to the company's core purpose, and
- Performance metrics that focus on functional abilities.

Irrelevance

Market forces (technology, competitors, regulations, customers, or some combination of these), can alter the fundamental economics of the business so that the core purpose is no longer viable. Sometimes these changes come quickly, but these forces usually act over an extended period of time, sometimes ten years or more. The indications of good cultural health are very straightforward: healthy companies see the threat and listen to the outside voices warning of peril.

A healthy company notices when the world changes. The rise of a "disruptive" competitor and/or technology is often visible, even if not completely understood. Leadership might be concerned and confused about what to do, but they understand the danger. For example, the internet grew quickly but did not spring up full grown overnight. Newspapers today see they are threatened by the online news sources. Most saw this fairly quickly, even if they were not sure what to do about it. The music industry grasped the peril of free file sharing almost as soon as it began and moved to stop it, bumbling badly until a combination of new technology and business models solved the problem. To go back to buggy making, vehicle ownership grew over time in a world once dominated by horses.

Given the huge increase in information available today, there is no defense for missing these signals, especially considering they are loud and explicit. Many voices often note that the world is changing and that companies must adjust. There are always false prophets, but there are also plenty of reliable signs. Healthy companies listen to these signals.

Unhealthy companies often fail to see the signs that are apparent to outsiders.[1] The company argues with its critics but does not listen to them. Critics are dismissed as enemies when the company is too insular. An unhealthy culture acts as a distorting filter, bending information into the most favorable light. In a stream of mixed signals that is 80% bad and 20% good, the latter are grasped and widely displayed while the ominous signs are ignored or downplayed.

Loss of Founder

Sooner or later, the founder of a company leaves.[2] Some professional managers will understand the value of the company's core purpose and keep it strong, but most will be less committed than the founder. They may even be hired to manage the "excesses" of the founder. Sometimes the passion that drove the founder is seen as a neurotic if endearing tendency needing to make way for professional-

---

1   Zook, Chris. (2007). "Finding Your Next Core Purpose," Harvard Business Review.

2   Schein and Kotter have both noted the importance of the founder in driving the mission of the company.

ism and a focus on business. So decay begins. Steve Jobs commented that technology companies begin to die when sales people and bean counters start making the decisions.[3]

There is another side to this: the founder's ways can become ossified into binding traditions. Failure is usually analyzed and spurs change but success does not. Winning breeds complacency and comfort in the status quo. Since the world always changes, this can be even more damaging than drift. The original intent of the founder is lost but the superficial ways he managed the events of his time are enshrined as "how we do things" and becomes part of the formal and informal processes that define the culture. This stops people from sensing change and stifles innovation. Tradition clouds people's visions and ties their hands instead of providing guidance and drive.

New Recruits

When companies grow, they recruit people (often from business schools) who want in on the profits. These new cohorts may like the focus of the enterprise, but not as a consuming obsession. Their commitment is intellectual, not deep and emotional. They drift away from the original intent as they rise through the ranks and assume positions of influence.

Performance Metrics

Performance metrics sometimes aggravate drifting away from the company's core purpose, insisting on formal metrics, focused on "performance." They seldom touch on how well the employees understand and further the company's true reason for being, as the people doing the measuring do not understand it themselves.

Professional management, recruits, and human resource departments are all necessary to grow a company, but these natural forces work against a strong core purpose. The company can lose its rudder and forget its reason for being. The disappointment with Apple's Lion is attributed by some to the company's loss of focus on digital designers as their primary customers.[4] Numerical evaluations of a business are easy to carry out but do not sustain healthy cultural values.

---

3   Pontin, Jason. "Microsoft and Apple in a Tough New World," Financial Times, October 29, 2012.

4   Garfinkle, Simon, "Review: Bad Apple," MIT Technology Review March 20, 2012 http://www.technologyreview.com/printer_friendly_article.aspx?id=39925.

4.2 Symptoms

There are some clear signs that a company's core purpose has lost its ability to guide the enterprise, summarized in Table 4.1.

Area	Unhealthy	Healthy
Shareholder Value	Shareholder value stressed by management. Explicit management of short-term fluctuations in stock price. Focus on cost reduction.	Focus on great products and services. Shareholder value is an outcome of proper focus.
Organizational Stability	Constant restructuring	Continuous improvement
Business Model Stability	Senseless drift to diversification. Promised synergies that never arrive.	Sensible diversification
Mission Statement	Unclear, long, lofty meaningless, generic	Clear, concise, meaningful, inspiring
Project Framing	Unbounded, always looking for greener grass, not implementable. Politically motivated.	Focused on business, with implementable solutions

Table 4.1: Symptoms: Core Purpose Decay

Shareholder Value

When the core purpose of a company is working, the focus is on producing relevant products and services for customers. Shareholder value is an outcome of a well-run company; management ignores short run swings in the stock price. People focus on the company's objectives, products, and customers and the company keeps a steady course.

When the core purpose has been diluted, leadership stresses shareholder value and tries to manage short-term swings in the stock price, often done by cutting and delaying important programs to manipulate quarterly earnings reports. There is much talk about how to reduce costs, not how to produce something customers love. This is the behavior of executives who are no longer creating shareholder value. They lead their companies into a wilderness with no idea how to get out. They are desperate to make it through the next earnings conference call. Outsider can see this from press statements of the CEO and the annual reports.

Organizational Stability

When the core purpose of the company remains a guiding light, organizational changes are driven by business needs. They are usually minor – tweaks for continuous improvement.

When leadership has lost sight of its mission, they show affection for constant restructuring. The cliché describing this behavior: moving around the deck chairs on the Titanic. With every new disappointment comes a new restructuring plan, often with special charges against earnings. These "one-time" charges occur again and again.

Business Model Stability

In a healthy world, the business model is stable and diversification is sensible and part of a strategic and operational road map. Cisco is an example of growing profitably through acquisitions. Disney grows profitably through evolving business models. When these companies diversified their offerings, the reasons were clear and met external approval.

When the core purpose has lost its ability to guide, there is a senseless drift toward diversification. The company goes into unrelated businesses that make little sense in terms of customers, abilities, or products. "Synergy" is promised, but the words are all high-concept and the benefits are always down the road. Managers look everywhere there is a glimmer of a higher margin or investment banker's promise. The track record of companies trying to change their position in their industry's value chain is dismal, yet the surface story seems compelling when the metric is return on assets or margins. Why shouldn't a chemical company become a bottler? The short answer is that they lack the ability to manage a business they know nothing about. But good judgment evaporates when the core purpose has faded and no longer provides a rudder.

Mission Statement

An enterprise's mission statement is a good signal of the health of the core purpose. Some examples of healthy mission statements come from IHG and post-bankruptcy GM. A few years ago IHG, a global hotel company under new management, changed its mission statement to "Great Hotels Guests Love." Here is GM's post-bankruptcy mission statement: "To build and sell the world's best vehicles." The new statements are clear, concise, and specific to the business. They tell people where to focus and what they must do well. The words are backed by the full and honest intent of the company's leadership.

The best example of this is from politics, not business, and is Winston Churchill's speech "…We shall fight on the beaches, we shall fight on the landing grounds, we shall fight in the fields and streets, we shall never surrender." As one commentator wrote at the time: "…One of the reasons why one is stirred by his Elizabethan phrases is that *one feels the whole massive backing of power and resolve behind them, like a great fortress; they are never words for words' sake* (emphasis added)."[5]

When the company's core purpose is drifting, the mission statement is illusive and meaningless – a clear sign the company has lost its way. An example is "We will put our customers first, become global leaders, act with the highest standards of integrity, provide opportunity to our employees, and give a good return to our shareholders." This is all great stuff, but these words have little value in driving action or providing focus.

A variant on this symptom is when the company's mission statement is long, committee written, and no one can remember it. GM's mission under its failed management was: "GM is a multinational corporation engaged in socially responsible operations, worldwide. It is dedicated to provide products and services of such quality that our customers will receive superior value while our employees and business partners will share in our success and our stock-holders will receive a sustained superior return on their investment." The words are meaningless corporate gobbledygook to the point of comedy, albeit tragic comedy. None of the words were true, ironically; it is a statement of what they were not doing.

Project Framing

In a healthy company, projects are focused on real problems and are well framed. The analysis of alternatives is rigorous and the chosen path is one the company can implement. Major endeavors tend to go well, driven only by the complexity of the work.

---

5   Manchester, William and Reid, Paul (2012). *The Last Lion: Winston Spencer Churchill: Defender of the Realm*, 1940-1965. Little Brown.

A weak core purpose leads to poor framing and misguided alternatives in managing daily operations. People tend to frame efforts as a reason to move away from the core business, under the "grass is greener over there" theory, and lose focus on fixing the underlying problems. There is often little guidance placed on how to bound the alternatives, so projects are likely to founder or shift. There is little ability to keep the right course and, even worse, little understanding of what the right course should be.

As companies analyze reasons for a decline in business, they are likely to do the math on the basic cash flows correctly. But they will often miss subtle but essential elements needed to be successful, such as supporting processes, capabilities, structure, and instrumental cultural values. The cash flows and 5-year plan might look enticing, but the problem shows itself during implementation. Implementation will often fail as people make recommendations at odds with the core purpose, and the supporting instrumental cultural values, processes, and structure. "Great idea, we just can't build it" is a common refrain.

The illusion of gold at the end of the rainbow leads people to follow foolish and fruitless paths.

4.3 Senior Management Remedies

Managing the core purpose of the enterprise is the job of the Board and the Senior Management team. They can take actions to see the threat coming and manage it in a timely way.

In this Section, we will discuss six senior management remedies for decay of a company's core purpose:

- ♦ Long range radar: the ability to look ahead and see a distant threat,
- ♦ Debate, dissent, and decentralized decision making ensures that people who see the threat are heard,
- ♦ Peripheral becomes core: tangential abilities form the bases for new businesses and purpose,
- ♦ Broaden the offering: integrate separate categories into broader services and solutions,
- ♦ Reposition: find different customers for existing products, and
- ♦ Mergers and acquisitions: buy or merge in a way that creates a new business model.

Long Range Radar

Long-range radar is an important weapon against becoming out-dated. This can take many forms, from reading to talking to "gurus" to formal market research. There are many places where a company can put its ears to the ground including technology, customer tastes, rising competitors, and government regulation. Some companies do this quite well – they are able to manage today's issues while making sure there is a tomorrow. Many of these business leaders read and have a sense of history, geography, politics, and culture, both high and low, in the traditional sense of the word.[6] According to Charlie Munger, Warren Buffet spends half his time reading, mostly in widely different fields. This might be bucking a trend of declining reading in society as a whole.[7]

Debate, Dissent, and Decentralized Decision Making

Debate, dissent, and decentralized decision making enable a manager to sense distant threats. Voices of concern are much more likely to be raised and heard if debate and dissent are expected. Within the company, some outposts will meet the threat first. If they are able to speak and are listened to, the odds of a surprise go way down. Decentralized decision making means the company's "sensing" powers are distributed over space and subject area, providing another channel for information into the enterprise. It also gives a portfolio of perspectives, rather than just one.

Here is where the role of middle management is critical. *They are on the "front lines" and need to take responsibility for making sure that the people at the top understand the presence of threats.* The analyst who tracks technology and reads the working papers out of MIT might be the first to notice that his company's IP (intellectual property) will be obsolete

---

6   Coleman, John. (2012). "For Those Who Want to Lead, Read" HBR Business Blog, August 15, http://blogs.hbr.org/cs/2012/08/for_those_who_want_to_lead_rea.html.

7   In a recent National Endowment of the Arts Survey on reading, it was noted that reading has been declining for the last 20 years. Between 2006 and 2009, for the first time, there was a reversal of that trend for all age groups except 45-54 year olds, the age of most managers. See "Reading on the Rise: A New Chapter in American Literacy" (2009), National Endowment for the Arts, http://www.arts.gov/research/ReadingonRise.pdf .

in five years because someone just received VC funding to develop new technology. He needs to be able to get the word up the chain that change might be coming.

Great companies are not fated to die because of changing currents – many adjust. Vigilant and strong-willed companies have demonstrated the ability to change many times. There are at least three ways companies can change their core purpose successfully:

♦ Turn a peripheral ability into a core one,

♦ Broaden the product's appeal, and

♦ Reposition.

Peripheral Becomes Core

One path is to take a peripheral part of the business and make it core. Intel switched from chips to microprocessors and IBM changed their focus from hardware to services. Xerox switched from copiers to document services. Another good example is Western Union, which changed from telegrams to moving money. Fuji switched from film to digital, brought its film expertise to bear for LCD flat panel displays, and then built a cosmetics business based on chemicals used in its film business.[8] These examples involved wrenching changes in the business, built on existing but fringe competencies.

Broaden the Offering

Another path is to broaden the product in a way that changes the value to the customer. Disney is a notable example. They managed to integrate their offerings of theme parks, movies, hotels, and merchandise to offer an "entertainment package." Instead of selling individual "categories," they targeted the share of entertainment wallet and revitalized their business. Energy service companies have done the same. They were threatened by new competitors and customers that wanted to insource their services. The response of the major service companies was to bundle their offerings and sell "well-management solutions."

---

8 "Kodak is at Death's Door; Fujifilm, its Old Rival, is Thriving. Why?" Economist, January 14, 2012.

Reposition

A third path is to find new customers for existing products by "repositioning." The best example is how Mars, working with Saatchi and Saatchi, changed Snickers from an old and tired brand of candy for kids to an energy pickup for young professionals. The product stayed the same, including the packaging. Yet the product redefined itself and became a tremendous success.

These companies succeeded, but others failed. Eastman Kodak was a company with all the advantages but failed to adjust to the digital age. Like Fuji, Kodak had a near monopoly position in its home market and forecast the rise of the digital age early on, but decided not to move into digital because digital was less profitable. Kodak tried a minor foray into pharmaceuticals but failed and spun off its chemical division in the mid 90's as a non-value added activity (Eastman Chemical, market cap as of August 2012: $8 billion). Kodak had a deep sense of complacency, brought on by its long-term success and near monopoly position in the film market. The difference between Fuji's transformation (market cap as of August 2012: $8 billion) and Kodak's failure (market cap as of August 2012: $50 million)[9] is their culture.

British Petroleum thought to redefine its core purpose under the leadership of Lord Browne and became BP (Beyond Petroleum), a "sustainable" energy company. Due to spills, fatal accidents, and then the Macondo blow out, this was seen as an insincere marketing and public relations (PR) program (even before Macondo, the effort was seen as little more than PR). This disaster was widely attributed to BP's culture of cost cutting. Now BP means Back to Petroleum, but the company is in retreat globally. In the last 10 years, its stock price remained flat while Chevron's increased 230% and Exxon's 178%.

Sometimes there is little one can do, even with the best culture and management. Retailers used to win by offering one-stop shopping but they are now threatened by on-line stores. Their response is to shift emphasis to smart phones, tablets, and service, but they are struggling and they may not survive.[10] Wikipedia has mortally wounded encyclopedias, including very good ones such as Germany's Brockhaus.[11]

---

9   As of September 29, 2012 for all three companies.

10 Zimmerman, Ann "Can Electronics Stores Survive?" Wall Street Journal August 30, 2012.

11 "A Chapter in the Enlightenment Closes," Financial Times, June 14, 2013.

Newspapers seem caught in an unavoidable bind and many local daily papers have closed – having lost their monopoly on news and local advertising, they could not find a formula for survival.[12] They seem to be today's buggy makers.

Mergers and Acquisitions

This is the favorite response of many companies despite poor odds of success. Clayton Christensen and his colleagues pointed out that 70% to 90% of acquisitions fail. The acquiring companies are typically confused about the reasons for their purchase and usually do a poor job of integrating the new company.[13] If managed properly, M&A can make sense as a way to improve a peripheral capability or to broaden offerings. The failure rate, however, should be a strong caution flag.

Summary, Senior Management Prevention of Core Purpose Decay

Fortunately, top and middle leadership can keep the core purpose strong and useful as long they recognize the problem and have the will to tackle it. The actions of Senior Management boil down to two key actions:

◆ Recommitting to the core purpose, and
◆ Clearing out the issues leading to the drift.

These two actions can lead to deep and sometimes painful change.

The main cure is for leadership and the Board is to recommit to the core purpose, tune it up if necessary, remove the causes of decay, and put in place the support to keep it strong. Apple and Toyota are powerful examples of how this was done by bringing back the founder or a member of the founding family. GE and Xerox are good examples of how it was done by insiders.

Toyota is an interesting case that is not as well known as Apple's. In 2009 and 2010, Toyota was faced with unprecedented recalls and quality problems due to aggressive expansion that valued growth over keeping the "Toyota Way." The legendary founder, Eiji Toyoda (aged 95 at the time) stepped back in, removed the CEO (although in the Japanese way) and 60% of the Senior Management of the company. He

---

12 Buffet, op. cit.
13 Christensen, Clayton et. al. (2011) "The New M&A Playbook," HBR March 2011.

installed his nephew, Akio Toyoda, who promptly reasserted the commitment to Toyota quality principles and promised expansion would never again be done at the expense of quality.

Apple's case is better known and understood. Apply brought a "professional" manager, John Sculley from Pepsi, to run the company. He entered into disagreement with Steve Jobs as Sculley decided the company should compete for the same customers as IBM. The Board and Sculley forced Jobs out. After eroding share and profits, the Board removed Sculley and, after several lackluster CEOs, brought Jobs back, who turned Apple into one the most valuable companies in the world by renewing the focus on "insanely great" products for the non-corporate market.

GE is a positive example of a company refocusing on its core purpose. Much of the refocus is due to the leadership of Jack Welch, who had come up from the ranks. After drifting into mediocrity under his predecessor, Welch recommitted to excellence and demanded every business must be in the top one or two in its field, otherwise the business would be gone. He then built Crottonville into the world's greatest internal management school. Under his leadership, GE became the most valuable company in the world.

Xerox's turnaround, led by insider Anne Mulcahy, was the most traumatic. She closed the underperforming desk top division, refocused the company on its core business of copiers and printers, slashed costs by reducing sales and administrative costs by cutting 30,000 people, but kept R&D and product development investments. While tremendously painful, it has been hailed as one of the great turnarounds.

In of all of these cases (Apple, Toyota, GE, and Xerox), recommitment to its core purpose led to changing people, streamlining the organization, and changing processes. While they differed in the degree of trauma, all experienced at least some pain. Businesses were cut, people were let go, efforts were redirected.

Another common theme of all of these efforts was a refocus on the customer of its core business. Often there was a public apology to its customers for going astray. GE was a bit different as it is a holding company, but it committed that each business would be either number one or two, or would be cut.

All of these companies put in place new systems to reinforce its renewed commitment. In their own way, each revitalized their radars and customer sensing abilities. One of the most interesting commonalities to all four is how they each brought in old keepers of the flame to restore the company. Apple's founder came back, Toyota brought in a member of the founding family, and "lifers" led the efforts at GE and Xerox.

They each began with a recommitment to the core purpose and then used that to transform the companies, each in its own way. Each involved pain, but all were successful.

4.4 Middle Management Remedies

Primary responsibility for fixing problems with the core purpose resides with the management committee and Board, but all managers need to:

♦ Support senior leadership,

♦ Control the problem in their day-to-day work, and

♦ Communicate issues up the ladder.

Managers can support the actions of senior management by helping them expel the forces that led to drift and make sure they do not contribute to them. Many problems will be embedded in the organization and will be visible to middle management, who can then raise the issues with senior leadership if they cannot solve the problems themselves. Everything that senior management does to remedy natural decay must be reinforced at lower levels.

Many strategic and operational improvement projects will be affected by natural drift and managers are responsible for bringing them back on course. Managers need to confine the framework and alternatives to those supporting the core purpose. This requires discipline and the ability to debate effectively. Done well, this can help solve the problem of a weakened core purpose by surfacing it as an issue during debates on a project's scope and increase management's awareness of business problems.

Another cure is to consider alternatives that are out of alignment with the core purpose but review these alternatives with upper management, including all the "soft" issues in the analysis. At least this way, people's eyes are wide open and they should be able to think seriously about the drift away from the company's core purpose. Sometimes one of these alternatives can result in a successful new business that can be kept or profitably spun-off. This leads back to the importance of healthy long-range radar and being alert to opportunities to broaden the offering.

5

Diagnosis and Treatment: Instrumental Values

We will briefly discuss this part of culture, even though we consider instrumental values the least important and best understood cultural value.

Instrumental values are like spice in food: they lend a distinct flavor to companies but have little to do with the nutritional value. There are many different ways of making a tasty dish and people enjoy different tastes.

These values align the specific business model of the enterprise with the surrounding environment, given a healthy core purpose and infrastructure.

> Edgar Schein gives an example about Northrup.[1] The engineers at Northrup were informal, quick to give feedback, hostile to hierarchy, and focused on technical excellence as their overarching value. The people at headquarters were hierarchical, formal, and overdressed – in other words, "suits." The reason was straightforward. The people at headquarters were constantly dealing with the military, which insisted on this type of behavior. The engineers had to deal only with each other and produce technical wizardry. Each behavior was appropriate and fit their different business needs.

The key word is "appropriate," which means "suitable" or "proper in the circumstances." A wide range of values will fit any particular circumstance. Honda and Toyota are different, as we noted. Exxon and Chevron, two of the oil and gas "super majors" display different

---

1   Schein, Edgar. (2010) Organizational Culture and Leadership 4th Edition, Jossey-Bass.

instrumental values. In industry after industry there are examples of companies with similar business models and markets who have a different "look and feel" or, in the original metaphor, taste. These differences can be important in attracting employees who sort themselves on the kind of work environment they prefer. Japanese who prefer traditional values apply to Toyota; those with a rebellious streak want to work at Honda.

This does not mean that the range of values is infinitely broad or that errors are impossible. Herman Kahn is reputed to have told a group of U.S. generals in the 1960's that there were many ways to win the Vietnam War and only one way to lose it; unfortunately that is what they had chosen to do. We have mentioned several companies where the culture contributed to demise, but not because of instrumental values. Mistakes with instrumental values are embarrassing, but not deadly.

Companies do need to be conscious of how their style aligns with their business model and the external world. This becomes an important issue if people move from one activity to another and differences exist. If working in Japan, the hot tub can be an important conference location, so one must be prepared for this.

6

Diagnosis and Treatment: External Focus

We have discussed core purpose and instrumental values and how these key aspects of culture can be developed and maintained. For the next four chapters, we'll discuss cultural infrastructure, beginning with external focus.

6.1 Forces of Entropy

People in small companies are close to the outside world. Even administrative assistants feel the boat rock from waves caused by customers, the economy, or bad luck. Small companies that lose focus on their customers are quick to die; large companies take more time. Assuming a company survives infancy, there are reasons the world becomes more distant. Time and success turn a small company into a large one and create distance between the employees and the outside world. This reinforces the fear many employees have of being exposed to the marketplace. Staffs such as Marketing and Government Relations can act as filters as well as conduits to outside constituencies. Wall Street can make matters worse by reinforcing franchise models. Finally, if a company is too successful, government will come in and threaten anti-trust action, driving the focus inward.

To summarize, forces of entropy relative to external focus include:

- ♦ Size: the larger the company, the greater distance between management and the customer,
- ♦ Fear of the marketplace,
- ♦ Specialized staffs (e.g., Marketing, Government Relations) control access to the outside world,
- ♦ Capital efficiency demands from Wall Street pushing towards franchise models, and
- ♦ Anti-trust threats when a company is too successful.

Size

As a company grows, leadership grows more detached from the world; people at lower levels are even more isolated. This is a simple and obvious statement, but important for understanding one of the most powerful forces degrading corporate culture. The customer is no longer everyone's responsibility. The management committee views the customer as one its many tasks, not the only one. The CEO and top managers will seldom mingle with customers except with the largest (or the most glamorous, if the business is lucky enough to attract that sort). Small companies are like commando teams stuck behind enemy lines; everyone gets the mission and knows what must be done for survival.

Fear of the Marketplace

The marketplace terrifies many people within major corporations. They dread the thought of selling something as either beneath them or frighteningly outside their competence, akin to solving multivariate differential equations. Customers are abstractions, not real, and there is little intuitive understanding of them. This is true for nearly everyone who works in large companies. These people want safety, income, an interesting job, and a pleasant work place. Large companies are armies, where only a small part form the pointed end of the spear and the rest are support and rear echelon and want to keep it that way. Recognizing this, some companies do all they can to force their workers to meet with customers.

At MacWorld Expo a few years ago, Apple had a huge display at the show, and dozens of Apple engineers and programmers – not sales staff – in their Apple golf shirts were on the floor. You could tell many were uncomfortable having to talk with "real" customers – *but they did it.*

Specialized Staffs

The marketing and sales activities of large companies require dedicated staff, including market research activity. The marketing and sales staff believe it is their job to "own" the customer and they are accountable for "customer metrics." The larger the company, the more "professional" these staffs, which are proud of their ability to "interpret" the "voice of the customer" for the rest of the enterprise. Market research grows as a separate department, full of people pleased with their talent for understanding customers. Sometimes by accident but more often by purpose, they set themselves up as filters, seeing their role as a source of power and influence. Marketing/Sales/Research grow vested in having the rest of the company become distant from the customer, reinforcing the isolation of the enterprise, even though they would protest at this characterization. But even with the best of intentions, direct exposure to customers becomes confined to a few people within a handful of functions.

Capital Efficiency and Specialization

The demands of Wall Street for capital efficiency reinforce isolation. Hotels and food businesses have traditionally been a mix of owned and franchised properties. For reasons of "capital efficiency" and balance sheet strength, both have been pushed to reduce their owned properties and transition to a pure franchise business. Wall Street has rightly said growth is easier through franchising than direct ownership. But the franchise business model removes the company from its customers. No longer will company employees be expected to do a stint in the store or hotel where they can experience firsthand what the business means to the people it serves. Instead, they will focus on franchise owners as the "customer." While true to an extent, it is misleading. The relationship between owner and franchisee can be tense, as the two are always a bit out of sync. Company employees see the franchise owner as small minded and greedy, while the franchise owner considers the company employees ignorant and out-of-touch central staffers who have no clue about running a business. Mutual distrust and contempt are likely to follow.

Anti-trust Action Born of Success

Breakout, blockbuster success can be a terrible problem. When American companies dominate their markets, the Department of Justice helps by threatening to break them up if their success becomes any greater. This is strong inducement to focus on issues other than customers and was an issue in steel, computers, software, and autos. All these sectors saw their giants turn inward and then decline. Google is threatened today by anti-trust action in Europe and the US, even though it is free to use and costs nothing to switch to a competitor. People distrust big (wisely) and the political system reflects this long tradition. A wonderful Japanese saying: "the nail that stands out gets hammered."

6.2 Symptoms

Companies with an external focus understand their customers and are capable of producing inspired products and services. They are in touch with the world around them, and are able to sense and respond to external forces. When there is a need for a change, they see it and are willing to act. These companies play well with others and have good relations with their allies, suppliers, and distributors. They are positively engaged with civil society; debates might be loud but are seldom angry. Market-focused enterprises want government to establish equal rights and opportunities and a stable regulatory environment, but let the marketplace determine success. Leadership will reflect the diversity of the society around them.

When companies have grown to have an internal focus, the "us/them" dichotomy has grown too wide. People outside the company have become "them" and people inside are "us." This will always be true to a certain extent and can be healthy if kept within bounds. Being proud of your company and being part of the team is a healthy state of mind. When working well, a sense of team drives greater performance and a healthy external focus.

However, outsiders can become the enemy. Information stops flowing into the company as the gap acts as a self-imposed barrier. Insularity leads to choices made in an atmosphere of hostility to the external world, without the right information, but with extreme confidence. The outcome is mediocre products and services, complaining about failure, trying to recoup from government, and telling one another that all would be well with the world if only people understood.

Area	Unhealthy	Healthy
Respect for Outside World	Sense of entitlement combined with condescension	Believes respect must always be won anew
Products Hit Their Target	Mediocre products that often miss and seldom delight	Well-designed products and services that meet customer needs, occasionally inspired design
Sense and Manage External Forces	Deaf to important external forces and misses important threats and opportunities.	Sees external trends and forces and can manage them
See Need to Change	Sticks to the status quo for too long	Willing to change as external circumstances change
Relationship with External Stakeholders	Poor record of working with allies, suppliers, distributors	Plays well with others
Reaction to External Critics	Responds defensively to criticism by saying they are misunderstood and under appreciated	Mindful listening to external critics
Role of Government	Seeks legislative and regulatory remedies to market problems	Provides level playing field. Seeks solutions in the market place
Lifestyles	Leaders live in same neighborhoods, go to same clubs, churches, etc.	Diverse set of lifestyles

Table 6.1: Symptoms: External Focus

Table 6.1 summarizes healthy and unhealthy symptoms of a company's external focus.

Respect

When companies have a healthy external focus, they are respectful of the outside world and believe there is much to be learned from others. Customer and public support is something that must always be won anew, never taken for granted. Companies build trust capital with the world outside: with customers, NGOs (non-government organization), governments, and allies.

In an unhealthy company, past success leads to a sense of entitlement and arrogance. Unfortunately, this is combined with an attitude of condescension towards the outside world. Leadership may display a superficial amiability, but it is condescending: the grace of the aristocrat for the commoner.

Products Hit Their Target

When people inside understand people on the outside, they can identify with them, put themselves in their shoes and develop effective and, sometimes, inspired designs. The great consumer product companies are famous for the quality of their research and relentless customer focus. Fulfilling needs in new ways is much easier when you understand customers. When Japanese car makers first wanted to sell in the United States, they sent designers and executives to live with American families. Apple under Jobs was the poster child of the principle that deep customer understanding permits one to know what a customer will like before they know themselves.

Insular companies do not create inspired products. They may have a detailed product development process, but it is a crutch that substitutes for understanding customers, not an aid. Products will tend to the mediocre, competent perhaps, but seldom winners. They understand people just like themselves but are oblivious about people who are different. The company will have their greatest failures in the segments most different from themselves. The New Yorker magazine once had a map of the United States from the perspective of New Yorkers; it detailed Manhattan, showed some detail in the other boroughs, and then displayed an empty wilderness from the Hudson River to the West Coast.

Sense and Manage External Forces

Externally focused companies have a variety of mechanisms in place to sense what is going on in the outside world. These range from market research activities to senior leaders who are engaged in outside activities and who are in personal touch with external stakeholders. Companies that do this well can see and hear the world outside them. As a result, they can manage external forces by anticipating their impact on the business.

Internally focused companies tend to be deaf and blind. They fail to listen to their own research, to competitors, to outside trends, and to civil society. They do not see important threats and opportunities and do not pick up changes in tastes, new technologies, evolving public policy or novel competitors. People who bring up contradictory data during policy, debates are dismissed as weak willed and poor leaders. Market research is used to confirm wanted conclusions but dismissed when suggesting a different direction. The culture serves as a distorting filter for outside information, bending information into people's pre-conceived notions of the way the world should be, rather than letting them see how it is.

Insular companies dismiss competitors, particularly emerging ones (common derisions: Made in Japan, Made in China, Made in India...), and fail to identify them. IBM dismissed buyers of Apples as garage-based nerds and hobbyists. The Big Three dismissed buyers of Japanese cars as spineless "appliance lovers." An associate of mine related a story about a company that made x-ray film: one of their technical team leaders commented, "The Japanese make a better product than ours, and their price is lower, but we're not worried about that." Ten years later the company was out of business. Amazon killed Borders, but not Barnes and Noble (at least not yet), primarily Barnes and Noble later adjusted more quickly to the digital market place than Borders.

See Need to Change

Externally focused companies are willing to change when circumstances dictate. They do not zig and zag, but respond to external forces with deliberation. When the "constellation of forces" evolves to present a new opportunity, they see the chance and are willing to grab it.

Insular companies stick to the "tried and true" for too long. Managers decide the best path is to "keep on keepin' on." Product and demographic segmentation drive design and development and they produce products with incremental improvements over the status quo. Or they make what they would want, but not something driving passion among people different from them.

In the 1990's, which was not that long ago, I was working on engine alternatives for a sports car. The program manager and I were both concerned that there were no fuel efficient (but still sporty) variants being offered. The powers-that-be dismissed our concern by pointing out that surveys of existing customers showed that no one cared about fuel economy. This was true. The problem was that if someone did care about fuel economy, they bought another product. This is a self-inflicted wound, not the result of some clever competitor's scheme. These were not low IQ people, but their programming was wrong. They missed the true nature of the problem because it involved customers and external forces they considered alien. "Who would want a PC?" was IBM's early response to Apple. "Who would want to work on the Web?" was Microsoft's early response to the internet. "Who cares about quality?" was the response of all too many.

Relationships with External Stakeholders

Companies with an external focus find it easier to get along with others. They will have healthy relations within their supply chain – there will be the inevitable conflicts but not a perpetual state of animosity. Alliances with other companies will work well and survive over an extended period of time. Relations with civil society and NGOs will be intelligent, deliberate, and suitably engaged. Disputes will exist, but seldom in an atmosphere of acrimony. The government's role in the company's license to operate will be well understood. Differences of opinion occur but in an atmosphere of engagement.

In insular companies, the arrogance is a barrier to good ties with allies, suppliers, or distributors. The general attitude is "Who needs relationships?" combined with a strong drive to work through control rather than alignment and partnership. The company's attitude to outsiders is "They need us." The company will always want to win. Customers, franchisees and suppliers are viewed as entities for extracting value, not long-term partners; their role is to provide services, not be part of the family. They cannot carry out alternatives that need alliances and the support of other companies, government, or NGOs, because they do not understand or respect the needs of the many other parties critical to success. They do not play well with others and their allies and supply chain partners dislike them. They try to get what they want through coercion or purchase rather than from an attitude of mutual respect.

Reactions to External Critics

Companies with an external focus listen to external voices. Leading financial analysts are seen as informed and impartial. Business school professors are sources of ideas and valued criticism. Experienced reporters are viewed as sources of insight. Even shareholder activists are treated with respect (especially the leading ones such as Calpers).

Insular companies, in response to criticism, claim they are misunderstood and people do not appreciate the greatness of their products. They insist the solution is to speak louder so that people will understand. Problems are the fault of biased reporting and ideological critics who cannot understand the true value of what the company is laying before them. They will often cite their long tradition of greatness and past contributions as proof of the value of today's offerings. Outsiders are seen as enemies or friends, to be rewarded or punished.

Role of Government

Companies with an external focus see the role of government as providing a level playing field and stable regulatory environment. They do not want government in their business but know that governments matter and must be engaged. They see the marketplace as the field of battle and want government to make sure the deck is not stacked against them. Government will view the company with respect and invite its input in policy making.

Insular companies see the government as a prop against discontented customers, abused competitors, and angry civil society. In the face of continuing market setbacks, they will seek legislative protection and remedy. Effective lobbying lets companies avoid confronting their lack of market understanding. A utility executive once told me that one good lobbyist is worth a hundred good strategists. Those who espouse free enterprise seem quick to seek trade protection, tax subsidy, or regulatory relief when the market turns against them. Exxon has often sought government support for its foreign ventures and domestic problems, even while condemning big government.[1] One of the domestic car industry's chief lobbyists is married to the key member of Congress with oversight of their industry. Government will often view these companies as pigs at the trough: tolerated if necessary but not really welcome.

Lifestyles

When a company's leadership is engaged with the world outside their enterprise, managers and employees reflect diverse values and lifestyles. In a company town, the company is going to define the town,

---

1   Coll, Steve. (2012) *ExxonMobil and American Power*, Penguin.

not vice versa. But in other places, managers and employees live lives reflecting the world outside with respect to the neighborhoods, houses of worship, dress, schools, and clubs they choose.

When the company views the outside world as something alien, managers and employees become physically isolated. The "us versus them" attitude moves into physical and social separation. Managers of insular companies will live in the same neighborhoods, go to the same religious institutions, and belong to the same clubs. This social isolation reinforces the overall insularity of the company, as they seldom meet "different" people in their everyday lives (other than the servants, of course).

6.3 Senior Management Remedies

There is much literature on marketing and hearing the "voice of the market," but much of it seems unnecessarily complicated. The fundamental question is simple: does one care about customers and listen to them or not? The top leaders of the company and its working level managers can turn back the forces of entropy and keep the company focused on the outside world.

Senior management has the ability to maintain an external focus in a variety of ways. The first job of the leadership is to believe in the importance of an external focus and visibly model their belief. If Senior Management believes it is important for everyone to keep their eyes on the outside world, then people will behave accordingly. While there are important technical competencies in research and marketing, the issue is one of values; their own and those of their subordinates. It can be learned but not faked.

The following are actions appropriate for Senior Management to take:

- ♦ Experiential learning,
- ♦ Change those who are unwilling to change,
- ♦ Strengthen the marketing staff,
- ♦ Redefine roles of key staffs, and
- ♦ Change processes and metrics to emphasize outward focus.

Experiential Learning

A major task is to be clear on how you want people to change and help them to do so. For some, this will mean changing deep-seated habits. One effective way senior executives alter values is through experiential learning. Leadership needs to experience working with customers themselves. This can take several forms:

- An "immersion day" is a fruitful and fast way to get up to speed on customers. A variant on this is to "live with a customer for a day."

- Another approach is to listen to focus groups. Executives sometimes lose patience with these activities, since they are forced to listen and not allowed to talk. Yet they are a great way to learn. A report on the focus groups will have little impact, no matter how accurate and well written. To change a person's world view, the experience must be immediate and direct.

- If the business is business-to-business, then time with a buyer is time well spent.

This principle applies to other external stakeholders as well, although the importance of these will differ from company to company. Government and NGO's are important for commodity and energy companies, while specific customers are less so. With franchise businesses such as hotels and fast food restaurants, the senior leadership needs to spend time with customers and employees to understand them at a "gut" level and build bridges and trust.

Make Organizational Changes

The next task is to change those you must to transform the company's focus from internal to external. There must be a sense of urgency and only a little patience; bad actors need to go quickly. Some senior leaders will be the focus of the problem. An insular company is often dominated by one function that has become too powerful and overwhelms the rest of the enterprise. A proper balance needs to be restored, possibly requiring removal of the head of the activity and much of his or her team.

Strengthen the Marketing Staff

Perhaps the Chief Marketing Officer has been a lone voice in the wilderness and will be able to do a great job if the environment becomes more encouraging. Certainly the first choice would be to see if the CMO and the staff are up to the job. Our experience suggests it will be necessary to change the chief marketing officer and the director of research. They were likely part of the problem or too weak to fix it. Their replacements should then be leading the change in the rest of the organization, supported by the CEO. The too-weak and too-strong all need to change and then upper management and the board of directors must ensure the company stays in proper balance.

Alter Roles of Key Staffs

Besides the marketplace, other external groups that matter are government, civil society, and shareholders. These are usually managed by Public Affairs, Corporate Responsibility, and Investor Relations, respectively. Traditionally the role of these staffs is to make sure the company gets its way as much as possible. But this is an antiquated role. These staffs could also be responsible for representing their stakeholders' views to the rest of the company and helping the company understand them. The first exposure would need to be direct experience, not reports filtered by staff. Enlightened marketing chiefs understand this role, but it still has not permeated to these other groups, although there are some positive trends in this direction. The senior leadership must drive each group to work with each external stakeholder group to define problems and develop plans to fix them, then monitor progress and help clear road blocks.

Change Company Processes and Metrics

The top leaders must change company-wide processes and metrics to sustain external focus. Consider capital budgeting and personnel evaluation. Capital requests should incorporate research and show the impact of the proposed project on customers. This would help people focus on and consider the external world. The standard financial models used for project evaluation and product development need thorough examination. Deep in these models are numbers driving many decisions, often the wrong way. Their importance is poorly understood because they are well hidden and seldom discussed.

Human Resources should add a metric based on understanding of the customer and include it on the performance evaluation form. This might be harder to measure than functional expertise or standard management tasks, but customer understanding is a critical part of preserving cultural health.

These two changes together link an external focus to people's pocket books, through getting projects and programs approved (ultimately benefiting their careers) and directly through their performance appraisal. We are trying to change behavior and these are quick ways to do so.

6.4 Middle Management Remedies

Managers have a vital role in helping a company keep an external focus. Like the top, middle managers must believe and model the values and drive them into their teams. They are the ones making the business work day to day. Senior Management needs to help, but line managers and team leaders must then take responsibility for driving the values deeply into the organization. Like the top manager, the middle manager needs a team who can support him. The movie "War Games" has a wonderful scene where a computer "nerd" turns to his nerdy partner and says, "Remember you wanted me to tell you when you are being a jerk? Well you are." This is the spirit that will help all.

There are four areas where middle management can improve a company's external focus:

♦ Reorganize groups and teams who will not change,
♦ Lead experiential learning,
♦ Advocate and participate in benchmarking, and
♦ Be aware of problems that arise in framing, developing alternatives, and analyzing courses of action.

Remove the Wayward

Like the CEO, the manager may need to remove people whose values are unacceptable and who are unwilling or unable to change. The deeper one goes into a company, however, the more roles there will be for people who do not share the core values but do not erode them. Think about your IT person. It is preferable all these people "get it," but the company will be fine even if the person supporting the team's computers and printers is clueless about customers.

Experiential Learning

The role of experiential learning is as important at this level as at the top. Just as top managers need to understand the external world directly, so too must their subordinates. Middle managers will be focused on a particular segment or stakeholder.

Benchmarking

Benchmarking can be a waste of time – little more than a way to make sure you stay a follower or adopt a solution that does not work for your business. But for people who are focused internally, benchmarking can be a useful wake up call that helps them realize that the world is not the benign and safe place they imagine it to be. We are placing this as a tool for middle rather than senior management because benchmarking is useful at the level of components or sub-components, and standardized processes. These will be run by working managers.

Be Aware

The manager must be aware of how cultural problems related to external focus may impede his or her day-to-day effectiveness and needs to plan for them. Expect framing of problems to miss customer-centric issues, alternatives to be too mundane, and the analysis in danger of being weak. The manager can keep vigilant for these problems in major projects and normal business activity. Continual questioning helps make sure these problems are avoided.

7

Diagnosis and Treatment: Internal Trust

People within a company must work together to meet changing competition and markets. This cooperation cannot be scripted or mandated – life is too complex, too fast, and too uncertain. So the people who actually make things happen need to sort out the issues among themselves, without a detailed rulebook or a gun to their heads. For this to work there must be mutual trust in each other's competence and integrity, or business simply will not prosper.

The challenge for modern corporations is to maintain internal trust despite human nature, the size and complexity of the company, misaligned compensation systems, and pockets of incompetence. Internal distrust *never* makes good business sense. Management's challenge is to keep the company from splitting into a series of hostile fiefdoms, despite many forces that push in that direction.

7.1 Forces of Entropy

Internal trust has to be maintained in organizations as every internal boundary is a Petri dish for distrust and can create an "us versus them" atmosphere.

A small company is a band of brothers and sisters. People might not always like each other, but everyone knows each other's strengths and limits, making trust natural. Bad behavior is visible and easy to handle; people cannot hide behind others if they mess up or engage in petty conspiracy for self-gain.

One pillar of trust is understanding the ability and the motives of the other person. Is he more interested in the company or himself? Is he capable? Does she want me to succeed? Will she do as she says when the unforeseen happens? In a small company trust is easy to keep. Unfortunately, size and complexity come with success and, therefore, trust becomes harder to uphold.

Forces that lead to a weakening of internal trust include:

♦ Human nature,
♦ Size of the company,
♦ Organizational boundaries,
♦ Misaligned compensation systems, and
♦ Pockets of incompetence.

Human Nature

It is inherent within human nature to react first with distrust to someone who is, in any way, an "other." People forget that distrust and fear are natural and instinctive states. The "us/them" reflex is hardwired into our thinking by evolution[1] and manifests itself at every turn.[2] Even at early ages, children make these distinctions. And it is well documented that if you take a group and divide them randomly, each group starts to feel contemptuous of the other, even though they all know the division was random. This constant drive towards tribalism is a strong part of the human condition and is one of the major sources of cultural entropy. Except for a few saints, people's gut reaction to someone with a different label is defensive and hostile. We create so much ethical and religious philosophy pushing us in the other direction because our natural tendencies must be kept in check and consciously redirected. This also applies in the business world.

Size

Once a company reaches a certain size, it is impossible to know everyone and, as the company becomes larger, it becomes difficult to know even a small percentage of the people. There is some debate about the number of individuals we can know well, ranging from 100-300,[3] and how many we can know superficially, ranging from 250-500.

---

1   Wilson, E. O. (2012) *The Social Conquest of Earth*, Liveright.
2   Kahneman, Daniel. (2013) *Thinking, Fast and Slow*, Farrar, Straus, and Giroux.
3   There is a fair amount of debate about "Dunbar's Number," the number of people with whom we can have stable social relationships. The most recent estimate is ~150, with a range of 100-230. See Hernando, J et. al. (2009) "Unraveling the Size Distribution of Social Groups with Information Theory on Complex Networks," arXiv:0905.3704[physics.soc-ph].

But once a firm grows beyond 500 people or so, personal knowledge becomes impossible,[4] so the natural response is suspicion. This can be overcome, but only with effort.

Trust needs to be earned. Trust is won in two ways: personal knowledge or a trusted label. Size makes personal knowledge difficult and in business, there is no equivalent of a trusted uniform. If a man wears a uniform we have faith in, say of a US Marine, then we trust the man (or woman, increasingly, to their great credit). The people who wore the uniform have built up trust over time; trust is not just putting on a set of clothes. Effort and sacrifice went into building belief and it must be continually renewed. Activities with smart leaders can impose the necessary discipline and transparency to ensure their entire staff is seen as trustworthy. So being "Bob from Finance" is enough to earn at least the presumption of trust. Another proxy for personal knowledge is association with a "real guy." When old timers meet for the first time, they begin every conversation with asking whom they know, much like dogs sniffing each other. (Life would be easier if we could discover someone's trustworthiness through olfactory senses.)

Organizational Boundaries

Every company in the world has had to create an organization with internal boundaries. People talk about multidimensional matrices, networked companies and Nth Generation Management, but everyone draws boxes on charts and these divide the company into boundaries, which define borders of trust. If the units of the company are independent business units (like they are in GE or Berkshire Hathaway), each has its own internal boundaries and they compete with one another for resources from the central office. Managers compete for recognition and reward.

Transfer pricing, no matter how done, always seems to cause serious annoyance and resentment. This results in lack of trust between the business units.

Misaligned Compensation Systems

Compensation systems sometimes reinforce competition and discourage cooperation. Compensation systems are rarely perfectly aligned with company objectives and become less so as companies

---

4   On the other hand, Jack Welch claimed he knew his top 600 managers "intimately." See Crisp, Dave, "How Many People Can You Know Well?," Canadian HR Reporter, Nov 22, 2010.

become larger and more complex. Pinpointing individual contributions in team efforts is difficult and people can feel cheated by others they believe received the credit due to them.

Pockets of Incompetence

Pockets of incompetence grow in larger companies, as failed executives escape accountability through strong political connections or lack of senior management oversight. A backwater becomes a dumping ground for people who can't be fired. A senior leader's "special friend" is given shelter and sinecure. These become little pockets of cancer. Out of need, the rest of the organization creates "work arounds," usually involving some form of deception. The result is more distrust.

Monopolies and Oligarchs

Internal trust is less important if the enterprise enjoys great market power. When this is the case, the job of each group within the company is to get better and better at what it does; relations with other internal groups are set and stable. This might still be true in China, where state policy favors a few companies in each region and holds down internal competition, or in Russia, where oligarchs have a lock on economic life. We expect silos to be a big problem in companies in those countries and they will be a barrier to their global effectiveness. Russia exports only oil and weapons. No Chinese brands have a global presence.

7.2 Symptoms of Internal Mistrust

When there is a problem with internal trust, problems are not solved by hard evidence, vigorous discussion, and clear thinking. People do not debate in organizations where there is deep distrust – they fight, maneuver, and manipulate. Problems will be defined by finger pointing (when looking in the mirror would tell a more accurate story). An insular company is oblivious to outsiders; a silo-driven company is oblivious to itself. Table 7.1 below lists some of the common symptoms.

Information Flow

In healthy companies, information will flow freely within an enterprise. Information is the fuel for all good decisions, whether in creating new products, day-to-day operations, or the biggest strategic change.

Area	Unhealthy	Healthy
Internal Information Flow	Poor internal information flow	Information flows freely within the company
Internal Integration	Organizational silos with poor integration; functional dominance	Functions cooperate and change roles as needed
Conflict Management	Conflict ignored and suppressed	Conflict surfaced and managed
Work Processes	Shadow processes and "work arounds"	The formal processes are the real ones
Implementation	Poor Implementation	Timely and competent implementation

Table 7.1: Symptoms: Internal Trust

When decision makers in one part of the company need to know what is going on in another, they can find out. The finance people see market data and marketing staff understands the cost structure. Cross-functional committees have the relevant information they need. Team members may have different opinions, but all will have the same facts. People welcome data as the lifeblood to good decisions and want to make sure everyone in the enterprise appreciates the big picture and the details relevant to their domain.

In unhealthy companies, information often fails to flow across the organization. Information is hoarded and becomes a weapon to use against internal rivals. Leadership decision making is completed without all of the relevant facts and, more importantly, different world views. At the most basic level, how can the right decision be made without understanding how alternatives could affect customers, costs, operations, maintenance, and stakeholders? In a world with little change and only routine decisions, trust might not matter, but few live in this world. For the rest of us, business demands constant adjustment and this needs reliable information.

Davenport, one of the leading advocates of the power of information, stated the problem well:

> "Analytics can illuminate high-level questions about investment optimization, company strategy alignment, customer satisfaction, market condition influence, and key performance factors, *but only if decision makers can see across regions, business units, or*

processes and consider information from the enterprise perspective [emphasis added]."[5]

Note that Davenport does not claim good analytics will solve the culture problem. *On the contrary, the culture must be healthy to use analytics well.* This is why we refer to these cultural traits as "infrastructure."

Internal Integration

Healthy companies try to destroy internal silos. Divisions, sections, groups, and teams are able to trade-off local interests for the sake of the whole. Managers are willing to "take one for team," knowing they will be appreciated for doing so. Solutions to complex business problems require integration and tradeoffs across different functions and business units. In a seamless company, this comes naturally and the supporting analytics are sound. The most obvious example is the relationship between pricing, costs, manufacturing capacity, and customer demand. To get this right, you need to know how they come together to determine profitability.

Healthy companies make sure that everyone sees themselves as citizens of the company before they think of themselves as belonging to their immediate business unit. Most Americans pride themselves on other aspects of their identity. I have always been proud of my Jewishness and my Irish grandfather and consider myself a proud mutt. But like most Americans, being American comes first. In healthy companies, people feel the same way. Conflict will occur between parts of the enterprise, sometimes strong ones, but they are shaped by the different world views and perspectives, not Machiavellian plotting.

Internal distrust leads to poor integration. If manufacturing, marketing, finance, and labor distrust one another, capacity and pricing decisions will be the result of bureaucratic warfare. One of these might be the "winner," but the company will lose. Different organizations fight for power, often leading to one group dominating the others. When suggesting alternatives, people will not consider choices benefiting the "other guys," nor will they look at strategies that rely on cooperation. Alternatives requiring new ways of cooperating will not get put on the table, but people will happily look at choices that result in one group getting swallowed by another. The result is a warped perspective as the winner places its filter on the world. Every problem looks like an exercise in cost cutting if finance rules, or sales if marketing wins, or manufacturing efficiency if the plant guys end up on top.

---

5   Thomas H. Davenport, Jeanne G. Harris, Robert Morrison (2010) *Analytics at Work: Smarter Decisions, Better Results*, Harvard Business Review Press.

Conflict Management

When people trust each other, they are willing to surface issues and differences. Debate and disagreement take place within a context of solving problems and doing what is right for everyone. Arguments become heated, as they can within any happy family, but are driven by passion and respect, even love. Everyone understands the complexity of business, the need to sort things out, and the importance of surfacing issues. Difficult decisions need debate, in the old fashioned sense of the word. Points of view will differ about what to do, especially for the big questions. We get to a good answer by surfacing the differences and then figuring out what makes the most sense.

A paradoxical problem with distrust is that it buries conflict. When there is distrust within an organization, conflict is hidden, not addressed. Healthy debate takes place on a foundation of trust and respect. When these are absent, debates become fights and the focus switches from beating the competition to beating your colleague. The overwhelming weapon of choice is passive aggression – promising to do things but then not doing it, with some excuse or other. Then when life goes wrong, there is finger pointing along with excuses.

Work Processes

Most companies possess well-defined work processes that cut across the enterprise, including planning, capital budgeting, order-to-delivery, safety, and so on. These work processes tell the different parts of the organization how to work together on important tasks that are a regular part of the business. In companies with a healthy level of internal trust, these formal processes are accurate reflections of how the work gets done. In the best companies, people are thinking about how to improve their processes and working actively with one another to do so. Toyota is the archetype of a successful process driven company. Their recent troubles were due in large part to straying from these processes and their recovery is based on recommitting to them.

When there is an unhealthy degree of mistrust, the formal processes seldom reflect how people get the work done. People use shadow processes and "work arounds" in the face of the bungling and the untrustworthy. One coping mechanism is to create informal channels and improvised processes going around problem people and groups while still managing to get the job done. As a result there is the "official" way and the "real" way. This leads to complexity and extra work, at the least. Sometimes a process cop will step in and try to enforce compliance, not understanding why people are not doing the work the "proper" way. People nod politely and then do what they must to get things done.

Implementation

Some ideas are impossible to implement or carry more risk than the company is willing to bear. A company might decide to go forward anyway, but it should do so with its eyes wide open. When people within a company trust one another, they are willing to judge honestly their ability to execute the tasks and to negotiate with other parties to reduce risks and speed the effort. When doing something new, they work together in new ways. This requires trust and cooperation between the parties. Internal trust, therefore, can ensure that leadership knows what it is getting into with new projects and can manage implementation more effectively.

Poor internal trust across boundaries is a formidable challenge to the cooperation needed for implementation. Even if the project accurately frames the problem, considers the right alternatives, analyzes them properly, and makes the right decision, implementation failure can waste all the effort.

Have you ever tried to dance with someone who did not know how to dance? You either do your separate versions of the dance while standing far apart or take over the other person's movements. Neither is a recipe for winning the dance contest. In the movie "Royal Wedding," Fred Astaire dances with a hat rack and makes the hat rack look graceful, but unless you have that mastery, forget about it. Most of us require competent partners that we can trust!

7.3 Senior Management Remedies

There is a cure for distrust across organizational silos: the top level must decide they care enough to fix it, remove the underlying drivers of distrust, align incentives, and change the values that have become ingrained into people. The top level of the company must drive these. If they do not lead, middle management cannot fill the void. These actions can be summarized as:

- ◆ Fix the incentive system,
- ◆ Change habits,
- ◆ Appoint a champion to make it happen, and
- ◆ Avoid re-organizing.

Fix the Incentives

The reward system must align with other actions designed to change the culture, especially those concerning internal trust. Compensation has to build bridges within the organization, not reinforce castle walls. The compensation system needs to encourage leadership to make trade-offs that benefit the whole at the "expense" of their individual organizations. Accurate measurement and metrics allow a data-based understanding of how the company has gained and who has participated. Functional metrics, therefore, need to be integrated with assessments of how the work contributed to the whole. There must also be a fair and transparent way to adjust bonuses.

> When the compensation system is misaligned, it can have serious consequences. One friend of ours, working at a major chemical company, had performance metrics in the top 2%, but was given a mediocre rating. Her boss said they saved the top score for someone they wanted to promote. She found a better job rather quickly and left the company.

Change Habits

Once the incentives have been realigned, management must create an environment where working together is the norm and *becomes a habit.*

The problem is that behaviors have become ingrained and distrust part of the modus vivendi. Senior management statements will help, but only if managers are sincere and are part of a larger effort to fix the problem. Trust-building measures can help if the incentives have been realigned and leadership is serious. I am not proposing "kumbaya" exercises or going on camping trips together. These "team building" exercises do little to knit people together in the long run.

The most important team building exercise is to do the work, with honest discussion, slogging through issues together, planning, acting as a team, leavened by some social interaction. Beer helps.

There is a popular language of conflict management and conversational tools, developed by Covey[6] and Argyris.[7] By now most people in corporate life have experienced one or both, and no one can escape Covey's relentless commercialism. Despite the hype attached, both

---

6   Covey, Steven (1990) *The Seven Habits of Highly Effective People,* Free Press and associated derivatives.

7   Argyris, Chris (1993) *Knowledge for Action: A Guide to Overcoming Barriers to Organizational Change,* Jossey-Bass.

have merit. Covey introduced his seven habits, one being "First seek to understand."[8] Argyris introduced the notion of the "ladder of inference" and "strong advocacy and strong inquiry."[9] All this is fine, but with a big caveat. These ideas only work with a tremendous amount of commitment, effort, and sometimes, expense.

They will not overcome the root values and problems driving mistrust in the organization, but can help change ingrained behaviors that are no longer relevant. A short workshop is a waste of time and will be seen, with reason, as one more failed effort to patch over a serious problem. The methods become a superficial, new-age approach to the untreated, underlying problems.

Appoint a Champion

A senior person must have the mission and ability to drive internal trust as a main value and remove the myriad of obstacles standing in the way. (A "guerilla" is the term some companies use.) Internal friction within a company is common and certain. Egos are large, people compete, and no incentive scheme is ever perfectly aligned. Long-standing habits die hard. But when this gets out of hand and becomes destructive, management needs to step in and fix it. Someone must oversee the change and be strong enough to hold people accountable and deal with the management committee.

Do Not Reorganize

Organizational remedies to distrust seem to be a reflex. The hope is a new organizational structure will destroy the silos and fix the problem. It seldom does, unfortunately. If the underlying drivers are still in place, then the only result is to disrupt the organization, destroying the informal networks that make business happen and tearing apart pockets of expertise. The new boundaries become new reasons for distrust. There is a literature on managing "n-dimensional" matrices, but at the end of the day, no organizational structure is going to be fully aligned with the work. Functional expertise needs experts huddling together. Processes require working together across functions. A customer focus means having a complete picture. Regional issues mean a geographic focus. *Managing the causes pulling people apart and instilling the right values is more fruitful than redoing the org chart.*

---

8   Covey, ibid.
9   Argyris, ibid.

The worst possible action a company can do is to call for more trust, engage in team building efforts, do silly acts like wear hats that say "One Company," but leave in place the root causes. This only makes conditions worse. People will get the message no one is serious about the problem and leadership is either hypocritical or thoughtless.

7.4 Middle Management Remedies

Middle managers will feel the brunt of problems in internal trust. At the management committee level, people pretend to play nice, but at the working levels the problems show themselves, especially in important cross-functional projects. The problems resulting from poor decision making will happen at this level (invisible to the top). No one wants to complain to the bosses that their peer does not want to play and isn't playing fair when he does.

There are three specific actions managers can take to help with internal trust:

♦ Strong facilitation,
♦ Commitment to change, and
♦ Trust-building through work.

Strong Facilitation

A remedy for managing work in this environment includes strong external facilitation.

I once led a company's channel managers through a strategy to redefine distribution. The managers did not hate each other, but they did view one another as being their biggest threats (with good reason, as their products overlapped). When I started working with them, I was firm in running the meetings and projects, with structured exercises, facilitated discussions, and controlled agendas. As the project went on, it became less and less necessary for me to do this as we succeeded in achieving key interim objectives. By the end of the project, I was sitting on the sidelines and the guys were talking like fraternity brothers.

The effort must be accompanied by someone senior overlooking the project and demanding cooperation, or at least a suspension of distrust, and keeping enough vigilance and pressure to make it happen. In the project I just discussed, the channel managers were aware a new Executive VP was going to step in with his solution unless he was given something good. This kept them focused and mitigated the game playing.

This will not solve the underlying malaise, but it does help the effort reach the finish line. This vigilance must continue through implementation, or defeat can be snatched from the jaws of victory.

Commitment to Change

Middle managers can take a major role in clearing away the trust issues and modeling trust with each other. They must commit to be part of the solution, not part of the problem. This can work if the problem is mild and the organization has committed to fix it. There will be many opportunities at a working level to engage in good behavior and encourage it in others.

Working Together

A powerful approach is to gather people who do not trust each other and help them work together. Trust will come from engagement and doing the work successfully. In an atmosphere of distrust, groups "throw work over the wall," which causes mistakes and reinforces distrust. Like the senior level, working together in the right way can help. There is a small industry around trust-building, from "sharing" at meetings to rope exercises to wilderness trips. These are designed to create intimacy. Our experience is these can be fun but generally have only small benefits. Everyone feels good about themselves and each other around the camp fire, but all bets are off when they come back to the office, where everyone reverts to their prior work habits.

On the other hand, working together helps. It reduces the "us versus them" dichotomy in a context that matters.[10] Sometimes silos are the result of lack of familiarity and/or physical distance. When this is the case, tightly structured workshops can help build bridges. It is important to manage these aggressively to overcome the initial barriers of distrust and associated habits. And just as it is true for the top level, beer helps.

---

10 Mark Mortensen and Tsedal Beyene (2009) "Firsthand Experience and The Subsequent Role of Reflected Knowledge in Cultivating Trust in Global Collaboration," Harvard Business School Working Paper 09-131.

8

Diagnosis and Treatment: Leadership

So much has been written about leadership that is seems a waste to write anymore about it. Most is off putting, pompous, and often silly. (One is not sure if you should channel Genghis Khan or be "emotionally resonant.") Leadership has received disproportionately too much attention at the cost of understanding other cultural issues of equal import. Yet it obviously matters, as much as reading the literature would have you wish otherwise. If leaders are chosen without merit, not held accountable, yet control all decisions and do not permit debate and dissent, then the company is sunk. This happens when effective governance is lost, but is relatively rare if simply because it so clearly leads to ruin. Someone – the board or takeover guys – usually steps in before the problem becomes terminal.

Yet leadership must be addressed, as it is an important part of a company's culture. Our model of leadership is simple and cuts to the essence of what matters. Whether Genghis or cuddles, these five traits define necessary and sufficient values for effective leadership:

- ♦ Accountability,
- ♦ Merit,
- ♦ Respect without worship,
- ♦ Toleration of debate and dissent while demanding discipline, and
- ♦ Decentralized and horizontal decision making.

Different companies will implement them differently. The qualities defining merit in a high-tech startup are different than those in a global manufacturing company, but the importance of advancement by merit is the same.

The Braes Paradox is a fun idea in systems theory that is helpful in understanding the role of leadership. The concept, backed by theory and evidence, is that adding a new and better roadway to a highway system can make traffic worse because everyone starts to use the new road and congestion follows.[1]

In basketball, this is called the "Ewing Effect." When Ewing sat on the bench, his team improved their performance. The reason is similar: without Ewing, the play is distributed more evenly among the other players, leading to better performance.[2]

"Strong" leadership likely has a similar impact, if "strong" means decision making is centralized in one person. The other players stop doing their part and all the forces of friction and opposition converge on the leader. In business, this would mean the great man's desk is far too overburdened for his intellectual capacity and available time.

8.1 Forces of Entropy

We will highlight three forces of entropy that weaken leadership:

♦ Distance between decisions and results,
♦ People flee accountability, and
♦ Niceness replaces accountability.

Distance between Decisions and Results

The first reason leadership loses its edge is the gap between decision and result grows in time and space and makes determining merit hard. In a company's early period, performance is easy to judge. Success and failure are clear and apparent to all. As a company grows, however, the space between action and result becomes greater and merit becomes harder to judge. Layers emerge where the company was once flat. Each of those layers is an opportunity for screwing up or placing blame. Companies expand into new markets, sometimes in distant places. A boss in New Jersey makes a decision for Singapore. East and West quickly point fingers at each other when the result is a failure. M&A activities are not expected to pay off in Day 1. Come day

1 Youn, Heyjin, Jeong, Hawoong, and Gastner, Michael. (2008), "The Price of Anarchy in Transportation Networks: Efficiency and Optimal Control," arXiv:0712.1598v4 [physics.soc-ph].

2 Skinner, Brian. (2011) "The Price of Anarchy in Basketball," arXiv:0908.1801v4 [physics.soc-ph].

1000 no one is around to take the fall, as the long chain of dominoes ends unhappily. Distance insulates the decision maker from accountability. It becomes easy to lay failure elsewhere and people grasp at the opportunity to avoid responsibility, as in the famous line, "Mistakes were made, but not by me."[3]

People Flee Accountability

People flee accountability and are desperate to "escape from freedom."[4] The need to flee autonomy (and associated risk) is innate to our nature. No one wants to be held accountable, people loathe debate and conflict, and are desperate to be part of the group . Natural leaders are a distinct minority of the population and a smaller minority still of people attracted to large companies. A small and growing company will attract people who are willing and able to fight and lead. As the company becomes successful, however, the struggle to survive subsides to the calmer rhythm of product development and budget squabbles. The people who join large companies want safety, otherwise they would join a small company, or the military, or the Peace Corps.

The positive side of people who seek safety is they are often strong team players that can push down their egos to work together and make big things happen. Large enterprises need them, just as large armies need their logistics support. The net effect is that most people are the frightened, not the brave. Many companies, finding themselves in this state, issue calls for more "entrepreneurship," harking back to the founders as a model of behavior. These rallying cries are a waste of effort because they are contrary to the nature of most people. These people need to feel safe to be effective and energized. This is not complacency, but comfort with colleagues and superiors.

Niceness Replaces Accountability

When employees flee accountability, managers have difficulty holding people accountable for their actions (especially for poor decision making). Managers believe that they are being "nice." However, over time, this becomes another insidious force weakening leadership. This is a problem with successful companies practicing long-term employment.

---

3   Tavris, Carol and Aronson, Elliot. (2008) *Mistakes Were Made (But Not by Me): Why We Justify Foolish Beliefs, Bad Decisions, and Hurtful Acts*, Mariner Books.
4   Fromm, op. cit.

GM's story is a good illustration of why a nice guy can finish last. Rick Wagoner is a nice guy and so were his predecessors (see Appendix III). However, running a successful business means keeping order in your company. Everyone has a natural tendency to think that his or her contribution is the source of all good things and that they deserve to be rewarded accordingly, but people need to be told "no" when necessary. Firm boundaries need to be drawn or conflict and political posturing will be unending. In the business world, *effectiveness* is important. When people talk of Bill Gates, it is not about what a nice guy he is. Jack Welch's nickname was "Neutron Jack" when he ran GE. Henry Ford was anti-Semitic and was at best an idiosyncratic person. But all these men were effective.

8.2 Symptoms

There are many symptoms of good/poor leadership; we will highlight a few. Table 8.1 summarizes the most important symptoms.

Area	Unhealthy	Healthy
Leadership Quality	Serially bad leaders	Consistently good leaders
Attitude toward Leaders	Reverence	Respect
Decision Quality	Wrong reasons drive problem solving	Decisions made for right reasons

Table 8.1: Symptoms: Leadership

Leadership Quality

The best symptom of healthy leadership culture is a series of good leaders. A good example of this is GE, which has specialized in creating excellent leaders and is a poaching ground for head hunters. On the other hand, the clearest sign of poor leadership culture is serially bad CEOs. Even the best of companies make mistakes in choosing the CEO, but when the problem repeats, the issue is deeper. Most failed companies finally died after a long series of botched bosses (and some CEOs manage to destroy more than one company: George Fisher had a strong hand in Kodak's demise before he went on to be the lead outside director for GM), although some were victims to changing circumstance (for example, many newspapers).

Attitude toward Leaders

In healthy companies, people respect their leaders. Everyone understands who the boss is and they treat the person in the top seat as worthy of the position (even if everyone knows in their hearts they could do the job better if they just had the chance).

In unhealthy companies, the respect becomes reverence and even worship. It is a bad sign when people talk of their leaders in tones of awe and as exalted men. Even when using their first names, the tone is a bit pretentious, a false impression of equality and just being one of the guys. Subordinates speak the names with reverence, transforming "Jack" into "*Jack*." Respect is needed for effective leadership but here it is replaced by an unhealthy worship. Subordinates become weak and dependent, always waiting for the "great man" to solve their problems. Worship also plays into the worst traits of leaders, who are already short on humility.

Decision Quality

A revealing symptom of a healthy leadership is the quality of their decisions. The right issues surface and are sorted out properly. Complexity is handled well in Einstein's sense; problems are made as simple as possible but no simpler. Decision makers understand the nuances. They consider the right set of alternatives: neither too dreamy nor too stuck in the mud. Risks and uncertainties are part of the decision calculus and there is clarity on objectives and values. Implementation obstacles are well managed. When mistakes are found, people speak out and correct them.

Adjustment and midcourse correction are possible; people can change even as they move. Accountability ensures people take responsibility for their mistakes and work to fix them as quickly as possible. Most messes are joint productions, so each contributor works aggressively to correct course and engage in honest diagnostics about what went wrong and why.

When leadership culture is unhealthy, politics drive problem solving.

Lacking accountability, the leader frames issues the way he wants to frame them, whether right or wrong. While this might be the same as what is best for the enterprise, often it is not, at least in emphasis. A common self-serving frame is to play up the dire nature of the problem and magnify short-term issues while ignoring long-term concerns.

The problem will be presented as an issue caused by others. This gives the leader a chance to be a hero in putting out a fire but without any worry of punishment when the longer-term consequences land, as he or she will be somewhere else. People will avoid mistakes at all costs, which means avoiding meaningful action. "Kicking the can down the road" becomes endemic.

When leaders are chosen on some basis other than merit, they are likely to fumble complex problems. Mediocre leaders look uncritically to their own experience for the closest metaphor to the current problem and then apply the solution they think worked previously.

When decision making is too centralized and distant, the odds are the underlying issues will be missed, leading to unrealistic alternatives. The distance between decision makers and their subordinates and experts is large. Leadership is unapproachable and silence is the rule of the day. There will be little taste for engaging the boss in debate, even when in strong disagreement. Instead of many heads coming together, many heads are trying to mimic the boss. As a result, mistakes are made and, worse, go uncorrected.

A leader's maxim becomes a physical law of the universe. (Some have even published books of their sayings, the corporate equivalent to Mao's Little Red Book.) This is fine if the leader is always right, but that is not the way of the world. The leadership becomes the weakest link in a chain, rather than the creator of a resilient web.

Implementation is "easy" in a world without debate and dissent. People will march quickly to where they are told. The problem is the high likelihood of marching to the wrong place.

Therefore, a very common symptom of poor leadership is blaming others. No one will admit it when they make mistakes. I once did a retrospective on a failed engineering project at GM. This was a program that ended disastrously, not just a minor disappointment. The new team wanted to know what had gone wrong and wanted to make sure they did not repeat the mistakes (much to their credit). I interviewed the 20 people responsible for the prior program. Everyone was quick to point out how the others failed to meet their commitments but not one person admitted to making an error.

8.3 Senior Management Remedies

The responsibility for leadership culture begins with the board of directors and cascades down. This, of course, is one reason very bad cultures must be fixed by others, as self-repair would mean leaders removing themselves, something we never see. The quality of leadership must never degrade below the point where the incumbents can fix it without widespread resignations and retirements. Once it passes that point, the culture will spiral down to a terminal level.

Worship can go to people's heads and result in big egos. Debate and dissent can tax your patience. It is always easier to say "make it so" than to be a real leader. Our natural tendencies are towards becoming a bad leader, not a good one. However, these tendencies can be managed with will, effort, and discipline.

The following summarizes the main actions for Senior Management:

- ◆ Discipline and will (enforced by a strong board),
- ◆ Encourage respect and ban worship,
- ◆ Mandate debate and permit dissent, and
- ◆ Locate decisions correctly.

Discipline and Will

Accountability and advancement based on merit are a matter of will and work, not magic. The organization has to value these traits and fight off the forces of entropy that are always gnawing at it. The Board must do their job and insert spine into the organization. Accountability and advancement will cascade down naturally. If not, the natural tendency to avoid accountability and to advance friends will prevail.

Encourage Respect and Ban Worship

Avoiding worship is also a direct choice of the leadership. When leaders are worshipped, it is because they like it (even if they vehemently deny this). People who become CEOs are driven to do so. Few fall into the position by accident or because they are so much better than anyone else. They possess an overwhelming need for the top spot and are not happy with anything else. It is a short step to a sense of deep entitlement and self-worth the holder believes those around him should share. (We note in passing that this is a gender-specific issue and women leaders do not seem to have displayed the same desire to be worshipped. But it is still early for women in top spots in business, and let's not forget Leona Helmsley...) Worship is an occupational hazard of corporate (and political) leadership. The press aggravates the problem, as the story of "the great man" is much easier to tell than an in-depth understanding of a business. Worship is a matter of choice; there is little compelling reason for this trait other than as a motivator or way to justify triumphing over others.

Leaders need to create a feeling of safety for followers. People need to understand their boundaries, what they can and cannot do. It is the responsibility of leaders to create this, so people can work to the best of their abilities. When there is no sense of safety, then false niceness and conflict-avoiding behavior take over.

Mandate Debate and Permit Dissent

This is a second step to stopping worship. It is easy to mandate debate and dissent when making a decision, while demanding discipline after the decision has been made. Sometimes the behavior has to be modeled for those who do not get it. Meeting facilitation and formal rules help in companies where debate and dissent are unnatural. This must be done as part of the work, not as a separate training exercise. If done as training, the new values will be left behind when the real work begins. Meeting facilitation and formal rules are neither difficult nor expensive to implement.

Putting up a barrier is our natural and human tendency to avoid conflict. Most societies preach "good manners" and the importance of genial social relations. However, in a recent book on Israel's success in creating startups, the authors credit the military system of open and immediate feedback and criticism along with a natural culture that places minimal value on politeness for the success of its startups and its military.[5] We repeat the book's opening lines, a classic joke:

> "Four guys are standing on a street corner...an American, a Russian, a Chinese man, and an Israeli...A reporter comes up to the group and says to them 'Excuse me, what is your opinion on the meat shortage?' The American says, 'What's a shortage?' The Russian says, 'What's meat?' The Chinese man says, 'What's an opinion?' The Israeli says, 'What's "excuse me'?"

These behaviors must be implemented to the point where debate and dissent become habits and natural acts, which will take persistence and work.

---

5   Senor, op. cit.

Locate Decisions Correctly

Accountability makes decentralized authority natural. If leaders are picked on merit and held accountable for their results, there is little reason to take decision making away from them and every reason to leave it in their hands. Sometimes formal decision processes drive decisions far from the problems. If the local business unit must defer to the regional management committee, and the regional management committee must defer to the national committee, and they must in turn discuss it all with the corporate management committee, there will be a big loss in fidelity as information moves up and down the chain. The cure is straightforward: end this decision structure.

8.4 Middle Management Remedies

Managers dealing with poor leadership are handling the bad behavior of their bosses, which is no easy thing.[6] A manager caught in the bottom will be powerless if this is a large and global problem. If the problem is local and not too severe, many possibilities exist. The big strategic question is whether to confront the problem directly or to work around it. As we said earlier, the better path is to fix the root cause(s), but this may not be possible. Making a project succeed means finding a good solution, even when surrounded by systemic problems. Managers need to create safety for themselves and their people to function.

Actions are summarized in Table 8.2.

Confront cultural issue directly	Locate the work appropriately
	Offer respect, not worship
	Do the right thing
Work around the cultural problems	Do the work and give your boss the credit
	Separate the work from the organization

Table 8.2: Remedies, Poor Leadership: Actions of Managers

---

6 For a useful guide, see Bing, Stanley. (2003) *Throwing the Elephant: Zen and the Art of Managing Up*, HarperBusiness.

Locate the Work Appropriately

When work is overly centralized and too distant from the issues, the solution is simple:

♦ Include the right people in the effort,
♦ Make sure that the people understand the problem and your expectations,
♦ Consider the right alternatives,
♦ Include the proper local concerns in the analysis, and
♦ Address potential barriers to implementation.

The work should be located properly and be done by the right people. This might require some persuasion, but past failures can help make the case that something new should be tried. Given the ease of teleconferencing, this is more a matter of planning and will than of cost. While physical presence is preferred, even the most distant places can be accessed for someone willing to bend their sleep cycle.

Offer Respect, Not Worship

One cure is to confront leadership and to have the skill to challenge with courtesy. If the problem is not too severe and the degree of megalomania limited, treating leaders like peers, or first-among-equals, can be effective. Man up, act as a leader yourself, but show respect. People at the top are often tired of cowed subordinates, especially in healthy companies. A key to doing this well is to be right! Sloppiness, inaccuracy, and error will not be tolerated in this environment, so one must be "buttoned down" in the quality of the work. If the leaders smell fear, they will assume it means incompetence or insubordination and will act accordingly. Taking this path needs courage and skill by the manager, but that is all to the good.

Do the Right Thing

A good manager can create realistic "win/win" solutions, even in a hostile climate. The quality of the work will need to be more rigorous than normal if it involves solutions that are not to the immediate benefit of the problematic leaders. It is harder (but even more important) to do good work in a hostile environment. There are several ways to overcome meddling by bad leaders that can also help improve the underlying culture.

A useful tactic is to have multiple stakeholders from all the affected parts of the organization involved in project governance. They will serve to keep each other in check. There is the wisdom in the saying that when you have one boss, you do as you are told; when you have two bosses, you go crazy; when you have three bosses, you do what you want. Visibility helps drive accountability; murkiness lets people act badly. It also helps create trust across the silos as this governance structure provides a constructive way of working together on issues of mutual concern.

A more aggressive approach is to change the boss or isolate the bad boss. This is the boldest and best choice, if it is available. It deals with the real problem (perhaps permanently). Appeal to some higher authority to provide support for doing what is right. In one project, the team was having terrible problems with a Chief Marketing Officer. The CFO and CEO both supported what we were doing and helped us, but with constant tension and sniping from the CMO. This was ultimately resolved by the removal of the Chief Marketing Officer, which was a happy ending to a difficulty story.

Do the Work and Give Your Boss the Credit

While this sounds a bit cynical, it can pay to throw a sop to the leader who wants the glory, either by giving him credit, letting him make the presentation, or throwing into the final recommendation something he wants but does not compromise the core integrity of the solution. As lack of merit is often accompanied by laziness, these people are happy to cede the work, as long they believe they will benefit in the end. This is a dangerous path, however, as one never knows when mediocrity will exert itself in a damaging way. But these people are usually content to go with the flow as long as they believe it will carry them along. The outcome of the work is right, although the underlying cultural problem remains.

Separate the Work from the Organization

Another way to get the work done is to create a "skunk works" – doing the work away from the organization to avoid its contamination by the whims of inept or excessively impatient leadership. Pioneered by Lockheed Martin in World War II,[7] this is a good way to get to a well-framed recommendation with the right alternatives analyzed

---

7   See http://en.wikipedia.org/wiki/Skunk_Works.

well. The problem comes during implementation, when the project may fall apart. Unless the proposal is to carve out a new business and organization, the effort needs to be brought back into the company. The battle has merely been delayed if the recommended path goes against existing policy. Failing to bring people along during the development of the idea risks rejection; leaders do not like surprises that counter their beliefs.

Another problem with skunk works is they do not help the rest of the organization improve their ability to innovate. When the project is over and the work assimilated into the organization, the ability to create something novel is not transferred back into the organization. Motorola created the Razr phone in a skunk works but was not able to duplicate that success.[8] GM used Saturn to create a skunk works but eventually it died when brought back into the company.

---

8   Richardson, Adams (2010) "Considering a Skunk Works? Think Again." HBR Blog Post http://blogs.hbr.org/cs/2010/09/considering_a_skunk_ works_thin.html.

9

Diagnosis and Treatment: Time Orientation

Firms seem to be either adolescent, adult, or senile. The adolescent is always in the current day. The future does not exist, nor does the past. There is only the "now." They neither save nor hedge their bets but connive to bend the rules for their immediate gratification. Combined with a false sense of immortality, this leads to bad outcomes for both teens and companies. Many of the short-lived internet companies displayed this characteristic because their founders were barely out of their teens.

For senile companies, there is only a (poorly remembered) past. They do not envision a real future and spend their time longing for the past, remembering who they were rather than managing who they are now. Some examples: Kodak spurning the digital revolution, the domestic auto companies belittling small, high quality cars, and IBM in the 1990's clinging to mainframes as their core product.

Adults balance yesterday and tomorrow. They save but can benefit from today's opportunities. Adults value their heritage but are not bound by it.

Does this mean time orientation is part of the life cycle of a firm? You are either young, mature, or past it? So is it fated to be wrong at the beginning and at the end? No, neither irresponsibility nor dementia are inevitable in business; they are only inclinations. There are many thoughtful, well-run young firms, such as Ebay, Google, Whole Foods, The Corporate Executive Board, and Starbucks. It is difficult to pass judgment on firms less than 10 years old; these firms are 10-20 (today's teenagers more or less). There are many robust older ones, including those who have successfully renewed themselves such as GE, IBM, Toyota, Delta, and IHG.

Time orientation is not commonly thought of as part of culture in the business literature, but is understood to be important in studies of national culture. We think time orientation is a critical part of the cultural infrastructure of a business that needs direct attention and management.

9.1 Forces of Entropy

The forces leading a firm to act as an adolescent or senile are a combination of its age and how it manages success and failure. Age influences but does not predetermine a company's time sense. Learning ability is more important. Both the old and young can fail to understand the lessons of success and failure.

Forces of entropy for time orientation include:

♦ Unexamined victories are seen as inevitable (adolescent orientation), and

♦ Inability to change due to insularity and silos (aged orientation).

Unexamined Victories are Seen as Inevitable (Adolescent Orientation)

The childish think that every victory means they should repeat what they are doing. They cannot disentangle how current circumstances differ from the past, nor how the future could be different than today. The leaders of the company let their victories go to their heads in a childlike way. This gets worse if there is a string of wins. Like a kid who successfully takes the big jump on his bike several times without getting hurt, he assumes that he is immortal and keeps on doing it until he has a severe crash. Instead of appraising the realistic dangers, these companies assume victory is easy and there is no reason not to keep on taking that jump. Then they crash, bewildered that the world is a dangerous place. They do not learn from their successes and set up their own failures.

Inability to Change Due to Insularity and Silos (Aged Orientation)

Firms that enter an ossified old age usually do so after a long period of success. The success leads to insularity and, often, internal silos. Information stops flowing from the outside and within the company;

all the arteries become sclerotic. The result is a severe diminution of their mental state. The company loses the ability to understand and adjust to the world as it changes. At some critical point, they fail to renew their products and business model. Then, when life goes south, they are bewildered and confused and start looking back to their past greatness, as they are incapable of dealing with today, much less winning tomorrow.

We see more senile companies than adolescent ones for a simple demographic reason: companies remaining childish suffer high mortality rates when young and no one hears from them. Those with dementia, however, have had long periods of success and established names. They are visible, often painfully so.

Neither the childish nor senescent are likely to listen to any of this. Our remarks are addressed to the "mature young" who want to live to responsible adulthood and the "young old" companies who see some signs of decay and want to address it. These remarks are also addressed to Board members and new executives who find themselves appointed to firms that display immaturity or senescence and who want to understand and fix the problem.

9.2 Symptoms

There are various symptoms of healthy and unhealthy time orientation, as summarized in Table 9.1. For many, the childish and senile display the opposite sides of the same coin.

Role of Experience

Healthy adult companies understand their history, its lessons, and its relevance for today. The past is always an important source of understanding complexity. Our natural instinct is to look for similar events in the past and use lessons from those occasions to guide us today. Adults recognize the past is only an analogy, not the real thing, and try to understand how today is different than yesterday. There is no magic formula for this and the smartest may still get it wrong, but the logic is clear. They make a proper evaluation of their losses and their wins. They understand the mistakes that led to bad outcomes. They do not turn victories into mindless processes repeated again and again. They are aware of their past, understand the implications for today, and do their best to act for the future

Immature companies repeat common mistakes because they never try to learn from others or from prior experience. They are too

Area	Unhealthy	Healthy
Role of Experience	Repeat mistakes of others because no one pays attention (Child)	Relevance and limitations of historical analogs properly understood; mistakes and successes understood and lessons incorporated
	Look only to the past for meaning (Aged)	
Role of Vision and Common Sense	Vision and action without sense (Child)	Balance vision and common sense; Vision drives action
	Vision with no action (Aged)	
Understand Profit Equation	Disdaining frugality (Child)	Frugality seen as a virtue; cost versus value well understood including "intangibles"
	Confusing cost for value (Aged)	
Discount Rate	Too low (Child)	Discount rate reflects opportunity costs of capital
	Too high (Aged)	
Innovation	Too much innovation (Child)	Proper Innovation
	Too little innovation (Aged)	

Table 9.1: Symptoms: Time Orientation

impatient to look at the past (or others) and they are confident that they can always come up with something better. Hence the sense of "déjà vu all over again" as one looks at the mistakes of the inexperienced. They have no memories to hinder them and no guidance for avoiding old traps.

The aged will always look to the past for meaning. History will always be the source of the frame ("This is Munich all over again," or, "This is Vietnam all over again."). People will shove the problem into an existing mold, regardless of the fit. When something genuinely new comes along, it will be missed, as IBM at first missed the PC. The internet was initially seen as just another distribution channel, not a disruptive technology. Their memory is full but their central processors have decayed.

Role of Vision and Common Sense

Adult companies use their vision to propel their core purpose. They have a coherent vision of what they want to accomplish that is ambitious but reasonable. These enterprises understand that vision and action need to be aligned and never lose their good judgment about what is doable and what is a dream. They will still dream, but see it for what it is. Dreams give breadth to their hopes; adulthood lets them know what is possible and how to propel innovation.

Adolescent companies have vision and are quick to take action without using common sense and fully considering the risks. These companies take bold steps into unproven technologies and develop business plans without any clarity on how to make money. This approach has failed time and again. Leadership shows a teen's bravado and dismisses criticism as the words of foolish parents and Cassandras. They confuse the basic sense of those who criticize them with lack of vision.

Aged companies create visions without action. The aged will engage in activities that sound bold but lead nowhere. There will be much "visioning," as the words always sound so good, but the vision substitutes for actually doing something. Emphasis will be put on gathering the "low hanging fruit" first, and "proving" an approach before tackling the difficult. This is sometimes accompanied by hiring big-name consultants to lead the exercise but ignoring their recommendations.

Understand Profit Equation

Mature companies understand the profit equation. They know the difference between cost and value and are not flummoxed by the notion that many values are intangible. There is an appreciation that costs can be easily broken down into small parts and subject to measurement while values are complicated bundles of attributes that are hard to disentangle. They do not rail at this or pretend it is not true; their mature perspective lends clarity to their thinking.

Immature companies seldom understand the cost side of the profit equation. They do not realize that it is there and that it is part of the calculation. They disdain frugality (as anyone who has raised children can attest). They live in the moment, so there is little value put on savings and self-control. The stories of crazy spending on parties during the height of the internet frenzy are legendary. There was belief that if we spend it, good will happen, and if we spend more, more good will happen. Most of those companies are gone. This behavior is hardly confined to startups; Wall Street bankers are also notorious for this behavior.

Aged companies tend to ignore the revenue side of the profit equation, sometimes ignoring it completely. One of the most common signs of senescence is undervaluing investment and confusing cost for value (i.e., thinking only about how much things cost). The classic "bean counter" trick of measuring tangible costs while ignoring "intangible" customer values yields unfortunate results in the marketplace.[1] It is a classic symptom of a company aging and is still depressingly common. Failure to understand value is tied to diminished expectations for the future and the need to have immediate payback. The focus on low hanging fruit means they miss planting what they need to harvest for tomorrow. GM had access to technologies that others successfully commercialized. GM did not take advantage of this because the new technology was inconsistent with their cost control mentality.

Discount Rate

Healthy companies use discount rates that reflect their real costs of capital with (sometimes) a risk premium. They view these rates as one of many inputs in calculating the expected return from investment opportunities. While important, it is seldom a point of debate. Everyone understands that a dollar today is worth more than a dollar tomorrow but everyone also understands that money needs to be reinvested to keep the company healthy. When there are risks in investment, they are surfaced and measured directly.

Both the adolescent and the senescent use the wrong discount rate. Adolescent companies assume too low a discount rate, as they never understand they have to pay for something. The notion of opportunity cost is beyond their grasp. Immature companies waste resources on frivolous things that would never pass serious scrutiny in healthy companies. There is little attempt to understand risks and incorporate them into decision making.

Aged companies use interest rates higher than the costs of capital, implicitly admitting there is little point in investing in tomorrow, reflecting their lack of belief in themselves. They will use discount rates as a proxy for risk. This is simply muddled thinking, as it confuses the time value of money for risk. It also hides the true nature of risks, rather than reveals them. The entire investment stream is undervalued but the sources of possible problems are not surfaced, so they are not dealt with. This becomes a good way to avoid challenging action. Sensible projects do not get capital and the company continues its decay.

---

1   A good recent discussion of this is Lutz, Bob (2011), *Car Guys vs. Bean Counters: The Battle for the Soul of American Business*, Portfolio Publishing.

Innovation

Healthy adult companies value innovation. There is no consensus in the business literature on how to innovate properly, so we cannot say any given amount is right or wrong. Clayton Christenson discussed the dilemma of the right mix of disruptive and incremental investments.[2] There is no right answer on how to balance these two needs. Healthy companies figure this out as best they can. Even adult companies will struggle with innovation. Unhealthy ones never get innovation right.

Adolescent companies always want something new and shiny. They love to innovate, but have no mechanism for managing when they need to stop and turn it into something tangible. They innovate for the sake of innovation, not to produce something useful; they are dreamers, not doers. They will spend without discipline and without ever bringing something to closure and implementation, which requires hard work and drudgery, not just dreams. While dreamers have their place, they should not be running a company (other than early-stage startups).

For senescent companies, actions will stick close to the status quo and reflect "the way things are done around here." Orthodoxy becomes important and constrains actions. These companies focus on fending off hostile competitors, customers, or regulators. Nothing needing bravery or change will be considered unless there is no choice. When companies lose their courage, they focus on avoiding death. To the extent actions go beyond sidestepping defeat, they will focus on recovering lost glory, but only by sticking to the tried and true. Innovation will be distrusted and new competitors will be dismissed. Policies, technologies, and people will be kept around well past their prime. After all, if it worked before, there is no reason it should not work now. Risks will be magnified beyond proportion as people will assume they can do little to control the world, much less make the one they want. For senescent companies, there seems little point to it at all, other than getting back to by-gone days. They will never allow something to become obsolete or permit creative destruction.

9.3 Senior Management Remedies

The Board of Directors is responsible for making sure that adults are in charge. The senior management team ensures that the company is in neither their first nor second childhood. They set the tone on

---

2   Christensen, Clayton. (2003) *The Innovator's Dilemma*, Harper.

the importance of innovation, investment, and thrift. If the problem is not too severe, senior management can help the company grow up or renew itself.

Remedies for poor time orientation include:

♦ Have a strong, outside board,
♦ Bring in "adults,"
♦ Manage the culture,
♦ Be exposed to new ideas,
♦ Assign champions, and
♦ Require "after action" reports.

Strong, Outside Board

A strong, outside board is a powerful guardian of proper time sense and adult behavior. A well-run company needs board members with deep, relevant experience and strong wills.[3] They will see if the management team is immature or doddering, if poor thinking clouds investment decisions, and if innovation is foolish or inadequate. These are issues that require judgment and wisdom to answer and the Board should be a great source for both. Cultural health starts at the top and works down. Adults tend to choose adults and, unfortunately, the adolescent and aged are more comfortable with their own kind as well.

One problem is that the maturity of management can be unstable as once it goes bad it tends to become worse, rather than self-correcting. This is one more powerful reason for managing a company's culture and time sense. The fragile nature of maturity is why the Chairman of the Board should be different than the Chief Executive Officer and there should be a certain distance between the two.

Bring in Adults

One action that boards take is selecting senior management. Google is a good example of how the Board brought in an "adult" to manage the company and who then turned management back over to the founders when they were capable of taking the reins.

Manage the Culture

Guarding against silos and insularity is an important duty for Senior Management (as we have already discussed). A benefit of an

3   Buffett, op. cit.

external perspective and an integrated enterprise is the free flow of information and world views, keeping the wheels of innovation properly greased.

Exposure to New Ideas

Senior Management needs to be exposed to ideas and issues evoking the possibilities tomorrow might bring. This can take the form of looking at innovative competitors, talking to customers who are rapid adopters, or hearing talks from futurists and scholars. Just as in understanding customers, leadership must experience these directly; they cannot be in the form of reports from staff. The latter could inspire curiosity but normally will not be enough to cause significant action. Learning must be experiential to shake up existing mind sets.

Assign Champions

The Board and CEO can help by making the senior management team accountable, especially the CFO and head of R&D. The CFO is the guardian of financial analysis. He or she should be appointed the champion for properly accounting for value and costs and keeping the balance between frugality and investment. The CFO controls the parameters used in financial modeling of investment opportunities, the handling of costs, and the measurement of sales and customer value (the latter done in collaboration with the Chief Marketing Officer). If they hold the right values and drive them into the financial processes, they can do a great deal to keep the company's time orientation correct.

The head of R&D has point on innovation. He or she has the charge of making sure the right balance is struck in innovation and that the portfolio of R&D projects have the right balance between near and long term. R&D also has the responsibility to make sure innovation is deeply embedded in the functions, not confined to the basement lab. Marketing, finance, and manufacturing each need to push innovation in their day to day activities and get help for efforts that cross silos or exceed their ability to execute on their own.

Demand and Support "After-Action" Reports

Senior Management needs to insist that operating level managers engage in serious learning efforts for both successes and failures. For most companies, the relevant place to study success and failures will be at the middle, but senior management must require this and support the effort properly. People must be rewarded for discussing what they did wrong and encouraged to understand the limitations of successes.

9.4 Middle Management Remedies

There are some important actions middle management can take. One is to support senior management's efforts to avoid adolescent and aged behavior in day-to-to day operations and to seek help when help is needed to do so. These actions include:

- ♦ Conduct look backs,
- ♦ Force forward-looking strategy,
- ♦ Be exposed to new ideas, and
- ♦ Use formal decision processes.

Look Backs

Most successes and failures take place at the middle level, so conducting "after action" reviews of successes and failures can be a great contribution to the company. In many places, admitting failure is avoided at all costs, especially if it means taking responsibility for it. And no one wants to dissect victory either – the preference is to take as much credit as possible and move on. But if senior management requires and supports these discussions, then middle management can ensure that lessons from the past are properly brought into the enterprise. People will be able to learn from yesterday while keeping their focus on tomorrow.

Force Forward-looking Strategy

The remedy to reactionary alternatives is to force forward-looking choices, to think about opportunities for winning big, and to consider actions with the potential to make a big difference. People often think of these ideas, but are reluctant to bring them forward if the atmosphere is hostile. A little encouragement can uncover a great deal.

Exposure to New Ideas

Like top leadership, managers need to expose themselves to ideas of what the future might be, although it is likely to be more focused on specific functions and areas. There is a wealth of opportunities for deep dives into specific areas, from marketing to innovative materials.

Formal Decision Processes

When people confuse costs and values, part of the cure is to make the cost and revenue assumptions clear and based upon evidence. Dialogue and clarity will help overcome zealousness and lethargy. Formal decision processes can be helpful if they are well grounded in logic and properly governed. A guided project structure based on best principles, evidence, and logic will help teams overcome lack of thought and reason.

10
Diagnosis and Treatment: The Basics

When you see a problem with the basics, it has probably been there for some time. If the culture has wide-spread troubles with laziness, misogyny, bigotry, and corruption, it is likely the company has always had these faults. They started out corrupt and became more so. Recent research bears this out. CEOs and CFOs with legal records are more likely to perpetuate fraud. A more subtle effect is that personally spendthrift CEO and CFOs, even those with a clean record, are more likely to have fraud reported in their organization.[1] Another study, using confidential IRS data, found that American companies with owners from countries with high corruption rates are more likely to engage in tax evasion.[2]

Even when the giants like IBM and GM went through their worst times, one did not hear of corruption. So it is not hard times that lead good people to make bad choices. The Enron story is more typical: dishonest from the beginning and led by the unethical. Success leads to further dishonesty as companies get away with it and take this as a license to keep going until they eventually get caught. Much of the banking industry seems to have also followed this path.

---

1   Davidson, Robert, Day, Aiyesha, and Smith, Abbie. (2012) Executives' "Off-the-Job" Behavior, Corporate Culture, and Financial Reporting Risk," NBER Working Paper.
2   DeBacker, Jason. Heim, Bradley, and Trahn, Anh (2011), "Importing Corruption Culture from Overseas: Evidence from Corporate Tax Evasion in the United States," Indiana University School of Public & Environmental Affairs Research Paper No. 2011-10-01, http://papers.ssrn.com/sol3/papers.cfm?abstract_id=1941412.

We doubt anyone from this kind of company is reading this book (and if you are, our first piece of advice is to find another job). Many companies, however, suffer some problems with the basics, either minor widespread issues or sometimes locally severe ones, so we will discuss the basics in more depth below.

10.1 Forces of Entropy

Societal ills show up inside companies. Many societies hold a legacy of prejudice against women and minorities and the effects linger for a long time in businesses in those societies. While the most odious of these symptoms have dwindled because of laws and policies forbidding them, some subtle versions of these problems remain, as they are ingrained in the beliefs of the people. "Casual" anti-Semitism is still the norm in some places, as are similar attitudes to other minorities and women. Jokes about women and minorities reveal true underlying feelings. Occasionally there is an uglier side: successful women who are attractive are routinely accused of sleeping their way to the top and African Americans who make it are said to be "affirmative action" babies.

10.2 Symptoms

Table 10.1 shows some healthy and unhealthy symptoms of the basics.

Area	Unhealthy	Healthy
Ability	Race, pedigree, age, and gender matter	Race, pedigree, age, and gender do not matter, only ability
Work Ethic	Hard work is belittled	Hard work paves way to success
Education	No ongoing education	Education is important and ongoing
Ethics	Corruption	No corruption

Table 10.1: Symptoms: The Basics

Only Ability Matters

In healthy companies, ability is what counts, not race, age, or gender. As a society we have transitioned over the last 50 years from de jure prejudice to where it is illegal and fading. There is a legacy from how people were raised as children and it will remain for a while, but healthy companies understand they need everyone's talents to succeed and work to make it so.

Finding qualified women or minorities is sometimes very difficult if not impossible, so this symptom must be addressed with some care. But when the top people are a sea of male whiteness, it usually means there is a problem.

> We know of one professional services firm with 50 partners: 49 men and one woman. The firm expresses concern about this and swears they are not bigoted or misogynist in any way. But they created a rule stating that a woman partner who takes a leave of absence beyond normal maternity leave for childrearing loses her partnership. They do not see the connection between this and their lack of women partners.

Undervaluing ability affects a company's ability to manage difficult problems. If the framing is complex, it is likely to be wrong, as the people doing the work are not up to the task. Analysis will be shoddy and mediocre, as the employees may not possess the talent to do it properly. Models will be primitive; there will be nothing needing analytical methods, e.g., probability, networks, fractals/chaos, or analysis of "big data." When it comes to implementing, it will be done in a rote way, but complex tasks needing mental agility will either not be completed or will be completed poorly.

Work Ethic

Healthy corporate cultures value hard work. It is always good to "work smart," but the smart know there is someone just as smart who is willing to work harder. Nations have different work ethics (just try to get something done in Europe in August). But workers in good companies know it will be impossible to succeed without hard work.

Business cultures that belittle hard work reflect the surrounding national culture and, like many of their peers, are caught in malaise and loss of competitiveness.[3] Problems will be framed to minimize the effort needed to solve them. The issue will be cast as something standard, open to easy repair. The alternatives will be simple to execute. The analysis will be oversimplified, avoiding complicated modeling of the complex or unfamiliar. No one will want to do the hard work needed for implementation and the chosen alternative will be simple enough for someone keeping banker's hours to execute. Everyone will want to lead and create "the vision," but no one will want to ferret out the right numbers, do the needed research, or develop a rigorous financial model. There will be over delegation, with a few at the bottom doing all the work. These attitudes will lead to progressively eroded positions, making success less and less likely, unless the markets are protected (which is often the case).

Education

In healthy companies, education is valued and is ongoing. Companies show their commitment in various ways, from onsite classes to paid leaves for pursuing advanced degrees. But the key is that people believe in its value and importance.

Unhealthy companies do little ongoing education and cut it first in a down turn. A company's attitude toward education will be obvious to anyone on the inside. Companies that value education encourage it, support it tangibly, and even require it. Companies that do not value education will only pay it lip service.

Ethics

Healthy companies are ethical. It does not mean that no one cheats on their expense accounts, but it does mean there is a foundation of honesty, integrity, and compliance with the law. When incidents happen (as they always will), there is little tolerance of dishonesty and it is quickly dealt with.

When ethics are weak, the criminal consequences are well known, as is the long record of the incarcerated. There is a more subtle and damaging impact on the quality of the day-to-day work. Work will be chiefly seen as a path to self-promotion. Self-serving alternatives will

---

3   A root cause of Western Europe's economic problems could well be in this
    area. See Rachman, Gideon. (2010), "Europe is Unprepared for Austerity,"
    Financial Times http://www.ft.com/cms/s/0/8b24504e-5c65-11df-93f6-
    00144feab49a.html.

receive the most attention and analysis will be done to support the desired outcome. Implementation will be characterized by short cuts, questionable deals, fighting for credit, and avoiding work. It is hard to do good work unless there is a strong ethical foundation. It is not just a morals question – it is a simple business issue.

10.3 Remedies

Keeping healthy basics starts at the top but is everyone's responsibility. The path is to not tolerate violations, choose the right people and, when necessary, outsource.

Zero Tolerance

There is a strong consensus that the remedy for fixing problems with the basics is a policy of zero tolerance, especially for sexual harassment, racism, and unethical practices. There is not much debate on this, at least in Western companies. The Board and the management committee set the tone and show the level of tolerance.

A widespread mild problem of ethics can be very difficult to manage. If everyone, including your boss, cheats on their expense accounts, this is difficult to correct. In the not too distant past, it was implicitly permitted to choose among female candidates based on their appearance. (We know of one firm that hired only gay or ugly women because the CEO thought they would work harder if they had no romantic distractions and he thought that they would never leave to bear children. Wrong on both counts.) But if there is a general understanding that self-serving lies, manipulative bureaucratic plays, sexual harassment, and backstabbing are the norm, exhibiting integrity will be difficult.

Much can be accomplished if the problem is local, even if severe. In our professional career we have encountered two major ethical problems: one involved misreporting of performance data and the other a cover up of sexual harassment. The recourse in these instances is to bring in authority, usually HR, Legal, or Audit (assuming these do not rise to the level of crime, in which case it is time for the police, although we have never encountered that and do not know firsthand of anyone who has). These are trying events but the path forward is clear.

Choose the Right People

Another important remedy is working with people who possess the right work ethic and disciplining those who do not. This will need some senior management support.

Outsource to the Competent

Another remedy is to outsource the project and its implementation to consultants or to some other third party. This is a common choice and is good for the consulting business but is probably not the best reason to hire consultants or contractors. Still, most professional consultants have benefited from this issue. Not surprisingly, those who are the laziest demand the most from those they hire to do the work. The best remedy is to have the work done by the educated and the competent.

This concludes cultural infrastructure and we will now move to discuss self-preserving mechanisms.

11

Managing Cultural Law Enforcement

In most societies, and all Western ones, people understand law enforcement. Penalties are clear and lawyers help if we are confused and police if we are foolish. Most of us go about our daily lives happily unbothered by the bounds placed on us by laws and regulations (except for speeding of course).

Corporate culture's law enforcement is usually unobtrusive because people internalize the rules and act within their bounds. Like laws and regulations, culture sets itself deeply into the work. A web of open and tacit rules shapes the business and upholds the cultural values of the company. Unlike the law, however, enforcement is subtler, embedded into rules on how the work is to be done. Often, people do not even think of these decrees and customs as cultural law enforcement, but they are. Managing culture is impossible unless one understands these constraints.

In the previous chapters we discussed how to diagnose and manage the culture. In this chapter we discuss the mechanisms culture uses to preserve itself. We thought it better to discuss them as a whole because the enforcement machinery cuts across the different values. There are similarities across companies in how culture maintains itself, but each possesses its unique ways. Spider webs share a similar structure, but they differ in detail. The guidance here is about where to begin looking for the web, with the clear understanding that every company possesses unique traits.

Most of culture's law enforcement lives in six areas:

♦ Financial resource allocation processes,
♦ Human resource processes,
♦ External communication rules,
♦ Internal communication rules,
♦ Process enforcers, and
♦ People.

These first two areas define what a company does with its capital and people. The next two specify how information flows between the company and the outside world and within the company. "Process enforcers" are those directly charged with ensuring compliance with company procedures. People internalize the rules, some deeply, and are walking cultural fortresses.

Our perspective differs from the way others look at how culture preserves itself. Most focus on the rules that decide whether you are part of the "in-group," especially the use of scorn and isolation to punish people who violate norms. These play a role in understanding culture but only a minor one. The behaviors are easily spotted and addressed.

The important parts of cultural law enforcement are embedded into how the business works. Sometimes these are explicit and clear, but sometimes the enforcement is in the details and nuances.

We will outline how the six factors reinforce cultural values. Just as the police have departments that focus on different kinds of crimes (narcotics, vice, traffic, and so on), these factors each tend to focus their enforcement on separate parts of corporate culture, and, as with the police, overlap exists. Table 11.1 summarizes how cultural law enforcement applies to each cultural value.

11.1 Financial Resource Allocation Processes

All companies develop ways of assigning financial resources to competing internal opportunities. They influence the company's culture, especially the true purpose, internal and external focus, locations of decisions, and time orientation.

Cultural Law Enforcement			Financial Resource Allocation	HR and Compensation	External Communication	Internal Communication	Process Enforcement	People
C u l t u r a l		0. Core Purpose	x	x			x	x
	External Focus	1. External Focus	x		x		x	x
	Internal Trust	2. Internal Trust		x		x	x	x
	Role and Qualifications of Leadership	3. Merit and Accountability	x	x			x	x
		4. Debate, Dissent, and Discipline				x	x	x
		5. Empowered		x		x	x	x
		6. Decisions Where They Belong	x				x	x
V a l u e s	Time Orientation	7. Forward Looking	x	x			x	x
		8. Frugality and Investment	x				x	x
		9. Innovation	x				x	x
	Basics	10. Strong Work Ethic		x			x	x
		11. Ethics		x			x	x
		12. Continuous Learning		x			x	x
		13. Ability Matters Most		x			x	x

Table 11.1: Cultural Law Enforcement

Rules for Eligibility

To what degree does the process filter out ideas that are inconsistent with the reason for being? Are these filters that keep out the "noise" of the irrelevant or do they allow every idea through and base funding decisions on promised margin? An effective filter will strengthen the reason for being. A filter allowing the irrelevant will lead to an undisciplined use of resources and a loss of focus.

Rules for Incorporating External Forces into Funding Proposals

Does the process mandate an understanding of the external world? If funding proposals must discuss relevant outside forces, the company's external focus becomes stronger. People will make sure they understand external stakeholders and will develop the capabilities, such as market research and competitive analysis, to do so. Without this requirement, people will shifts the focus to cost control, self-aggrandizement, and/or internal politics.

Rules on the Location of the Decision Makers

Are the decision makers in a position to understand proposals and give them the attention they need?

Kraft struggled with its Oreo sales in China. They moved the decision making to its Chinese subsidiary, which changed the product's composition, packaging, distribution, and marketing. Sales increased from $20 million in 2005 to $400 million in 2012.[1]

Standards for Cost and Revenue Calculations

Are both cost and revenue estimates done with rigor and integrity? The integrity of cost and revenue calculations reflects how they are viewed by the enterprise. If a company does not value frugality, the cost calculations will be shallow. The poor analysis reinforces the disdain for cost control. The same holds for the revenue calculations.

The Discount Rate

Is a reasonable interest rate used to discount future cash flows? Academics debate the proper discount rate without an agreement on the "right" answer. Rates that are too high will heavily discount future cash flows and rates that are too low will discount the present and the legacy of the past.

Use of Financial Heuristics in Funding Proposals

Do the analytical short cuts hinder evaluation of new ideas? This is subtle. Sometimes, assessing overall return can be made simpler by using quick estimates. These estimates can become misleading if the world changes and the assumptions the shortcuts are based on are no longer correct. The company will miss innovation and growth opportunities. In oil and gas for instance, the short cuts to analyze the

---

1   "Kraft Changed its Biscuits for China," Financial Times, June 3, 2013.

prospect for off-shore assets are completely incorrect for looking at opportunities that can be made viable using hydraulic fracturing. For this reason, some of the major oil companies were slow to invest in non-conventional oil and gas opportunities.

These are just some of the ways that financial resource rules affect corporate culture. A company that wants to manage its culture needs to understand the implications of its own rules. This is often the territory of the Chief Financial Officer, who may be skeptical about the importance of culture. Financial resource rules are likely to be alien territory for people who are concerned with corporate culture. Both sides need to work through these barriers and cooperate.

11.2 Human Resources and Compensation

Who gets hired, promoted, and how they are paid form a major center of cultural law enforcement. Financial resource allocation shapes future projects and products; human resource allocation shapes the people. Human resource processes guide the role of merit and accountability, empowerment, the reason for being, and the basics.

Alignment with Core Purpose in Promotion and Pay

Do these pay any attention to the person's support of the reason for being? If so, then the reason for being will be reinforced. If people who walk the company away from its mission are rewarded, then the core purpose will drift, as others will try to do the same.

Merit in Hiring, Pay, and Promotion

Is merit the number one measure? Are high performers who lack the right background rewarded? Just as important: are poor performers with the right background compensated according to their performance? This is, of course, the most important test of merit and ability in the enterprise. Everyone knows who is a good performer, who is a poor performer, who has delivered on their commitments, and who has not. Everyone also eventually figures out who has been rewarded and who has not.

The Role of Independent Action

Were people who acted as empowered rewarded or punished? It is hard to define independence of spirit but it is easy to spot. Is there room for these people in the company? Are they held up as heroes and part of the mainstream or barely tolerated and on the fringe? The answers to these questions go a long way to driving the level of empowerment.

Cooperation in Functional and Business Unit Compensation

In a holding company, this does not matter, but it does in a cohesive business. Does compensation punish or reward cooperation and integration? Incentives to cooperate reinforce trust. Incentives to compete foster distrust and strengthen silos.

The Role of Hard Work

Does the human resource process support hard work? If pay and promotion recognize the difference between people giving their all and those punching a clock, it shapes the culture of the company.

Continuous Learning

Are there tangible incentives and real opportunities for learning? There are many ways a company can reward continuous learning and encourage it. If there are neither inducements nor opportunities, there will be little value placed on it.

Ethics

Is bad behavior punished? Punishment supports the primacy of ethics, not reward. More ethical people are not paid more money. Ethics are not a matter of degree, but of presence. The important way the human resource process supports ethics is by removing the unethical quickly and without remorse. Ethics will decay if there is little enforcement or complicit approval of unethical behavior.

Human resource processes will differ from company to company and so will the way they act on culture. But they are important everywhere and, like financial processes, need to be understood if culture is to be managed. Unlike finance, however, most of the people who manage human resource processes are familiar with the role of culture and will often be willing to be champions of culture change. This is a two-edged sword that we will discuss further in the chapter on getting started and organizational placement of culture management.

11.3 External Communication Rules

These rules are important because they control how information flows into the enterprise. We are not focusing on who is allowed to speak to outsiders (that is relatively unimportant). Our concern is who is allowed to engage with the world outside the company and the nature of those relationships. These rules make an obvious impact on external focus but also influence the role of debate, dissent, and innovation. The external world includes many groups: customers, competitors, governments, investors, suppliers, distributors, allies, universities and innovation centers, immediately surrounding communities, provinces/states, and other countries.

The importance of external communication rules differs between companies. Commodity companies might not need to worry about customers, except in total, but many of the other groups will touch on their success. The links between these groups and the company decide the degree to which a company is an island unto itself.

Rules About who is Expected to Engage

Is engagement expected of most or is it confined to a few people? Are protocols set? In some businesses, everyone is encouraged to know their customers, possess a grasp of the marketplace, think about social trends, and be in touch with the world around them. Beyond encouragement are *expectations* that employees will bring this perspective into their work. On the other hand, some companies believe these matters are best handled by a few experts. These experts are trained to interpret the information and and feed it into the company to those judged to need it.

When General Motors hired Robert Lutz to improve product development, one of his first acts was to look at the market research, which he expected was being done poorly. To his surprise, the studies were first rate and accurately predicted the market performance of GM's products. But the researchers were not allowed to share the information broadly within the organization. He quickly changed the rule.[2]

Expectations on external engagement shape the daily behavior of people and the external focus of the enterprise.

External Information in Debate and Dissent

Is external information expected to support debate? A good discussion rests on shared information. As Senator Daniel Moynihan once said, "People are entitled to their own opinion, but not their own facts." Effective debate about implications is impossible unless decision makers enjoy equal access to external information.

External Information as Input and Stimulus to Innovation

Are people expected to study others and use the lessons to stimulate internal innovation? Not all innovation involves wizards creating new technology. Much of it is simply people constantly trying to do better, trying to improve in small and large ways how the work gets done. External stimulus can drive this: seeing a competitor, or another business, or even a piece of art that sparks an idea. If contact is restricted and information is heavily filtered, it will be difficult to have a healthy innovation culture. People will not see the need for change, nor will they be stimulated to.

Rules on engagement with the world outside the company play an important role in determining the effectiveness of corporate culture and the overall health of the enterprise.

11.4 Internal Communication Rules

Companies make rules that create an embedded understanding about how people talk to each other across levels and organizational boundaries. Both play a big role in internal trust within the enterprise, debate and dissent, empowerment, and innovation.

At one extreme, communications are restricted to formal channels matching organizational boundaries and the management hierarchy. Internal functions communicate through formal channels by those selected to do so. At the other end are companies that expect everyone to speak up to bosses and to interested parties elsewhere in the

2   Lutz op. cit.

company. Companies may have a range of communication rules within their enterprises, with some business units or functions having formal and set rules, while others are more freewheeling.

There is no right way. Freewheeling information flows can lead to chaos, the signal getting lost in the noise, and information arriving too late. With rigid protocols, correcting errors of omission and commission is difficult. Bad information might be sent and important information left out, with little chance for those who know better to fix the problem. This dilemma is closely related to the never-ending struggle to find the right organizational structure, a related problem without a universal solution. These rules are determined by the purpose and context of information flows. The important objective is that the *right information* reaches the *right people* at the *right time*. The culture and the business are hurt when it does not.

Honesty and Speed of Cross-silo Information Flows

Are people expected to share information with one another thoroughly, honestly, and quickly? Internal trust is based on getting accurate and timely information. If this is not the case, the results are suspicion, unwillingness to share information, and bad decisions. The web of trust holding the organization together is either strengthened or weakened.

Rules on Debate

Who is expected to debate decisions before they are made, and how vigorous is the debate? Internal information is as important as external information for effective debate. Shared knowledge of financial strength, costs, technology, and product quality is the foundation for intelligent discussion.

Rules on Dissent

Are subordinates expected to voice their dissent? There is a wide body of literature on the importance of subordinates pointing out errors by their supervisors. When the boss makes a mistake, people must to be able to say so. The rules on debate and dissent impact empowerment. If people can debate, then empowerment is reinforced. The opposite is also true: people will not feel permitted to act if they are not allowed to argue.

11.5 Process Enforcers

We are singling this out as a separate category because of its importance. In most businesses, there are groups with the responsibility for ensuring that people act in a certain way. Almost all companies have a staff dedicated to Safety to make sure everyone obeys the rules. There are people in Audit staff responsible for compliance with GAAP. Legal staff oversees ethics, often with HR. The latter are responsible for enforcing compliance with policies on sexual harassment and discrimination.

Beyond these obvious examples, there are groups responsible for making sure the work is done in a certain way. We have a friend at a Fortune 50 company whose main responsibility is to ensure compliance with the investment manual of the enterprise. At many companies planning staffs ensure that the "proper" steps are followed for investment and product decisions.

Collectively these groups enforce the culture by making sure people act in a certain way. If the culture is to be managed, these activities need to be understood. Unfortunately, they are often ignored, dismissed as "bureaucrats." They are indeed; that is the point. These groups' self-interest is keeping the status quo. They will, by their nature, do all within their capacity to uphold the existing culture, as it provides their reason for being.

11.6 People

People are one of culture's strongest pillars.

In strong cultures, people internalize the values and make them their own. There is nothing wrong with this. All great organizations have this characteristic, from the Marines to McKinsey to Google. The people within these organizations cherish the culture. This means that they will enforce it as a natural act. When they see behaviors or recommendations that counter the culture, they disapprove and find ways of stopping them. They will feel a deep emotional response, not just an intellectual one. These people become "culture carriers." The culture becomes a part of these people's psyche and they actively do all they can within their power to preserve it. These people will also resist cultural change as the values are closely tied to their self-identity. In strong and healthy cultures, these are the guardians of the culture and are important reasons for success.

Unfortunately, this is also true for unhealthy companies with strong cultures. We will talk more about this later, but it means that when radical change is necessary, there is literally no reasoning with these people, as the culture has become embedded into their emotions. This is why turn-arounds of companies with with bad cultures means removing people.

11.7 Understanding the Rules

One more issue to address is how you surface the rules once you know where to look.

Financial and human resource allocations are relatively straight-forward. These align with formal staffs, so people will be aware of how they are shaping the enterprise's work. They may not think of themselves as culture's enforcers, however, so those doing the diagnosis need to guide the discussions. These staffs may also fail to understand some of the effects of their actions, so it is necessary to talk to those on the receiving end as well.

External and internal communication rules are easy to surface, as people will know what is permitted and what is not. Wide ranging discussions will be necessary to control for local variation and the effect of individual personality.

Process enforcers can be deeply buried within the organization, but they are easy to identify once you decide to look for them. Like those controlling human and financial resource allocation, they may not understand their own importance as cultural guardians. They must be engaged by people who understand culture.

Identifying culture carriers can be more difficult. They tend to be those that most strongly support the status quo and are the most resistant to change. But they do not wear marks on their bodies. In positive conditions, they will step forward as natural leaders. In times of big change, they will be the ones dragging their feet. These are the ones who are convinced they are unique and no outsider can possibly understand them.

Projects reveal cultures constraints, especially ones attempting to do something different. They surface the law enforcement mechanisms because they create ideas that are atypical. They are trying to fight the law and the law fights back. The law does not always win (although that is the safe way to bet), but it does reveal itself. These efforts become diagnostic tools for understanding a company's culture and how it protects itself. People whose careers focus on projects will have great insight into the company and be valuable sources for diagnosing it. We talk about this more in the following chapters.

Cultural constraints are easy to find because people are aware of them, even if they do not think of them in those terms. When people do seemingly irrational acts, they know it and so does everyone else around them. The most important point to remember is that "irrationality" is seldom irrational; the behavior is sensible once the constraints and context are understood. Sometimes it is a combination of insanity and history (e.g., anything having to do with the Middle East), but normally the behavior is being driven by constraints.

The people engaged in the behavior understand the underlying causes. You need to go a few layers deep on the "whys," and sometimes people are so entrenched they do not see the fences around them, but eventually you find the reasons. These are the cultural constraints and self-preserving ways of the corporate culture.

12

Getting Started: Organizational Placement and First Steps

The way a company manages other enterprise-wide issues should be used as an initial model for managing culture. Most companies have a history of implementing cross-organizational initiatives. That history should guide how to manage culture. Safety, healthcare, and quality are comparable important issues that went from casual to active management. Each company should look to those lessons first to decide what is best for them.

Following are general recommendations on governance, assessment, and planning. Managing culture is an imperative falling outside the scope of any particular function, so there must be broad participation across the enterprise. Both senior and mid-level leaders must take part, so participation must be deep as well as broad. We will discuss how to begin for each level, just as we have for treating specific cultural traits.

12.1 CEO and Senior Management

The last thing any company wants to do is to create a new VP for Culture. Most large companies are complex enough and adding a new organization can just increase costs and complications. This is also the way many companies avoid doing something meaningful: appoint a new VP without much staff or authority but with a big and important sounding mission. This creates some publicity and lets everyone continue what they are doing. After some time the new VP disappears and is never heard from again.

Managing culture is a shared responsibility but there are some natural champions for specific cultural issues. The role of the champion is to lead the diagnosis, recommend the necessary changes, and then implement. This is summarized in Table 12.1.

The reason-for-being must be owned by the Board of Directors, as it is the highest level strategic decision of the company. The traits involving leadership belong to the Board and the CEO and fall there in most companies.

The Chief Marketing Officer needs to be on point on driving an external focus, certainly for customers. The head of Government Relations needs to be on point on managing relations with NGOs and Investor Relations must be the lead for investors.

The CFO and COO are the natural guardians of frugality and investment as well as being forward looking. The General Counsel is the natural owner for ethical values.

Internal trust across the silos is a vital part of culture, with a strong effect on the company's day-to-day operations and decision making. Therefore the Chief Operating Officer is the rightful owner. The COO is also the only one besides the CEO with the power to manage this.

HR and Operations have a big role and, after the CEO, responsibility for the greatest number of traits, including empowerment, work ethic, learning, and the primacy of ability.

Overall leadership should remain with the CEO and Board. Managing culture is about how to make the business more profitable by changing the reflexes and thinking of the operating people and streamlining processes they have to use. No one lower in the organization has the authority to do this. This does not mean that cultural issues should dominate the CEO's agenda – they should not. But he or she will be the one to make sure everyone else is doing their part and help them when they need it.

12.2 Getting Started

The process of managing culture should start with an assessment of the current health of the culture and progress to a plan for change. There are several parts of this:

1. Perform a direct assessment of the core purpose and cultural infrastructure. Done in a workshop with top leaders and/or in several workshops spread across the enterprise,

Cultural Trait	Primary Responsibility
Reason for being (Core Purpose)	Chairman & Board
Merit & accountability	Board & CEO
Debate and dissent without worship	CEO
Decisions where they belong	CEO
Forward looking	CEO and his/her staff
Frugality and investment	CFO, COO
Internal trust	COO
External trust	CMO/Government Relations/ Investor Relations
Ethics	General Counsel
Empowered	COO, HR
Strong work ethic	COO, HR
Continuous learning	HR
Ability matters most	COO, HR
Innovation	R&D

Table 12.1: Suggested Responsibilities for Specific Cultural Issues

this should begin with a simple judgment of each piece. The evaluation needs to address each item. The discussion surrounding those judgments should provide insight into the causes and severity of the problem, adding depth to the direct assessment. The workshop and interviews should work on uncovering the core processes in the company that are reinforcing cultural problems.

2. The champion of each cultural area should assess which of the symptoms are present. This can be done as part of the workshop and through interviews.

3. Conduct individual interviews with long time members of the company and newcomers. The lifers hold a deep knowledge of the issues but may have assimilated the values so deeply they are no longer conscious of them. The newcomers will lack depth but will see the importance the issues missed by the old timers.

4. Survey employees' assessment of the culture and of the symptoms of cultural problems. Employees must be confident of their anonymity.

5. Conduct a retrospective on some puzzling failures where there is a sense cultural issues contributed to the failure. This will help reveal where problems are.
6. Put the results into a clear and concise description of the state of the culture, which will catalyze discussion by the governance group.
7. Create a plan to manage the problems surfaced during the assessment. This work has to be done by someone strong enough to challenge assumptions at all levels of the organization.

These steps may need to be done in several parts of the company if the enterprise is made up of autonomous units. If the parent enterprise is a holding company, then the focus should be on the problematic companies within the portfolio. The champion and governance committee needs to decide on the correct breadth of the effort.

It is also important that the plan begins with a few of the most important issues and addresses these issues thoroughly. A broad "shotgun" approach is likely to dilute the effort so much that little will be accomplished.

12.3 An Illustration

Figure 12.1 is a simple illustration of how managing a cultural issue works in practice. In this illustration, the diagnostics showed problems in internal trust, employee survey results and interviews showed the same, and there had been several implementation failures the leadership team attributed to poor cooperation between business units.

The leadership team decided that internal trust needed to be improved. After some investigation, they realized that their capital-allocation process pits business units against each other and, for historical reasons, joint projects are not permitted. The compensation system uses relative ranking, further aggravating competition and distrust. The business units are also deep organizational silos, with little cross-rotation of people. Communication is confined to formal exchanges. To make the situation worse, two of the business unit chiefs dislike and distrust each other. HR surveyed the employees working for these two managers and found that both had disenfranchised employees who did not trust their business unit head.

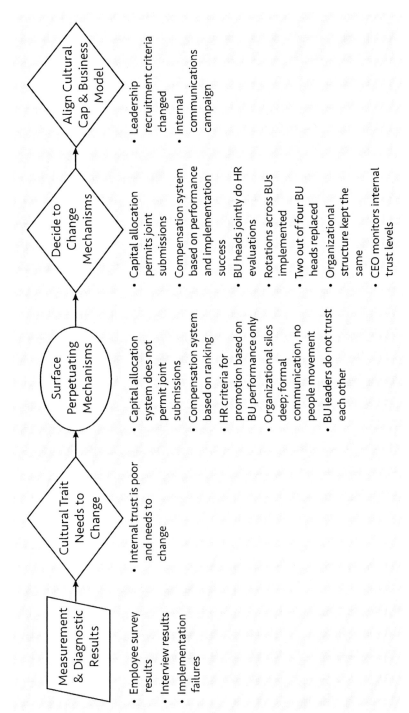

Figure 12.1: Cultural Change Illustration

In response, all these causes were eliminated, except for the organizational structure, which the management committee felt needed to stay in place. The CEO did remove the two business unit heads, said he was personally watching the situation, and expected real improvement. He also encouraged informal events attended by members of the different units. Only minor change was needed in the rest of the cultural capital and none in the firm's business model.

12.4 Managers

For managers, the steps to start are similar, but are on a smaller scale. For most companies, the champion would focus on the entire enterprise. The exceptions are companies with self-contained business units (e.g., GE). For these independent business units, their top leadership corresponds to the CEO level in the more general case.

The working level managers, whether in an integrated enterprise or standalone business unit, would start in a way similar to the top leadership. The steps would be:

1. Assess cultural health of the overall enterprise and how it affects their activity.

2. Assess cultural problems within their unit and their impact on the unit's objectives. These assessments should be done with less formality and resources than the one done for the company as a whole. A workshop should include the manager and his or her team. They should look at the list of symptoms discussed earlier and see if they are present. This will surface most issues. Have the workshop facilitated by someone who is not part of the activity.

3. Sort the issues from the first two steps into those issues they can manage themselves, issues they can manage with the help of others, and issues outside their sphere of influence.

4. For those within their control, they need to decide which are the most important and develop a plan for addressing them. The plans for managing these issues need to be detailed and have specific roles and responsibilities, with oversight and follow-up.

5. Issues needing cooperation with others need to be prioritized and then jointly managed with the relevant activity. This will require agreement between both parties on the nature of the problem and the priority.
6. Issues outside the control of the manager need to be referred to the champion at the top level of the company.

Many cultural issues can be, and should be, handled by managers, but they need to be done without disrupting the ongoing business and set up to provide genuine progress. This will make everyone feel included and encourage further engagement.

13
Changing a Strong but Unhealthy Culture

When the culture is strong and dysfunctional, there will be no big, internally driven changes. Anyone suggesting cultural change will be disregarded and even punished. The required major changes will be done only in a turnaround or bankruptcy, led by outsiders. IBM,[1] Continental Airlines,[2] Alberto Culver,[3] Xerox,[4] GM, and many others found themselves in this situation.

The people who led those turnarounds all said changing culture was a critical and immediate need.

♦ "Establish a results oriented culture ... Build a new corporate culture. A healthy culture is simply ... honesty, trust, dignity, and respect" – Continental

♦ "Novell had a dysfunctional culture, a sick culture ... a culture of fear ... and it was a big problem." – Novell

♦ "In addition to cost cutting, innovation, and growth ... the fourth requirement for transformation is culture change." – Siemens

---

1 Sellers, Patricia. (2008) "Power Point: 5 tips from IBM's turnaround champ," Fortune, http://postcards.blogs.fortune.cnn.com/2008/07/17/power-point-five-tips-from-ibms-turnaround-champ/ Also DiCarlo, Lisa. (2002) "How Lou Gerstner Got IBM To Dance" Forbes, http://www.forbes.com/2002/11/11/cx_ld_1112gerstner.html.
2 Brenneman, Greg. (2000) "Right Away and All at Once: How We Saved Continental," Harvard Business Review OnPoint Enhanced Edition.
3 Bernick, Carol Lavin. (2001) "When Your Culture Needs a Makeover," Harvard Business Review.
4 Birger, Jon. (2004) "Xerox Turns a New Page," March 16, Money Magazine http://money.cnn.com/2004/03/16/magazines/moneymag/stocks_xerox_0404/index.htm.

◆ "It's all about culture. You have to transform the culture, not just the strategy. Culture is what people do when no one is watching ... Culture isn't just one aspect of the game; it is the game." – IBM

They each created reforms to make their companies more customer-focused, remove silos, improve decision making, and so on.

13.1 Change People

An action common to all the turnarounds is replacing people. The changes were usually at the top but the one exception was IBM, where middle management resisted needed changes so many middle managers were removed.[5]

◆ "Clean House. The same team that leads a company into crisis is rarely able to get it back on track." – Continental

◆ "We ... replaced most of the executive management team, reducing seven layers of management to four." – Novell

◆ "If necessary, sweep out the old leaders ... Unfortunately in many cases I have had to fire them because they ... maintain their hope for some miracle solution and resist the rescuers in an effort to conceal their failure." – David James

◆ "At the top of the organization was a leadership team that really wanted to speed things up. The customer facing parts of the organization felt that the changes were the right thing to do. But there was a group of people in the middle that didn't want to have anything to do with it. They just wanted it to go away. They wanted it to be the way it used to always be." – IBM

---

5   The quotes come from the following:
Augustine, Norman R. (1997) "Reshaping an Industry: Lockheed Martin's Survival Story," Harvard Business Review.
Fryer, Bronwyn. (2001) "Leading Through Rough Times: An Interview with Novell's Eric Schmidt," Harvard Business Review.
James, David N. (2002) "The Trouble I have Seen," Harvard Business Review.
The HBR Interview, (2005) "Transforming and Industrial Giant: An Interview with Heinrich Von Pierer," Harvard Business Review.
Takeuchi, Hirotaka, Osono, Emi, and Shimizu, Norihiko. (2008) "The Contradictions that Drive Toyota's Success," Harvard Business Review.

Pieces of the organization with a vested interest in the old ways and failed leadership need to be quickly removed. Those who cling to the old culture need to go. There are few exceptions to this. The hope is that people see the error of their ways, but in practice they seldom do. There is no time in a crisis to coddle the stragglers who are impeding change.

This should be done as quickly as possible to minimize disruption. This turbulence is part of the company's transformation, but must not be a permanent state.

13.2 Respect and Confidence

People are removed to create a healthy organization where the vast majority can go on to thrive with successful and happy professional lives. It is no more callous than a surgeon who saves a life by the skillful use of his scalpel. Our son is a surgeon and we can say with complete confidence that compassion is what guides his hand, not coldness.

The turnaround's leadership will contain a high percentage of outsiders, including the CEO, but a couple of layers down and into the depths, most will be "old timers." Overall, most of the employees will be those who have been there in the past. They must possess the ability and passion to make the business successful and embody the cultural values of a healthy company. All of the people leading successful turnarounds said their main goal was to mobilize these people into a force for success, not to do it all themselves.

The first step to change must be a willingness to admit there is a real problem; this is a necessary step to health. The turmoil accompanying the changes should be held up as a victory to celebrate. Unless it is unduly protracted, its culmination can be seen as the end of the beginning and testimony to the survivors' ability to adapt and change. But it is good to remember that after Moses freed the Israelites from slavery, they complained about the food!

In a study of over 20 turnarounds, Rosabeth Moss Kanter found that restoring people's self-confidence and mutual respect are essential to the success of the effort. These were required first steps to restoring investor and public confidence.[6] The leaders "inspired and empowered their organizations to take new actions that could renew profitability. In short, each had to lead a psychological turnaround."

---

6   Kanter, Rosabeth Moss. (2003), "Leadership and the Psychology of Turn-arounds," Harvard Business Review.

Turnarounds take place in an environment of failure and anger. People are in deep distress, with self-loathing and mutual disgust over the bankruptcy / takeover. People in this state do not move; they hunker down and hope to survive. One of the first tasks of a turnaround is get the organization up and running again. Self-confidence and mutual respect enable people to work together, take leadership, and accept accountability. They also pump energy and get people to move.

Successful turnaround leaders understand this and make morale an explicit objective. Different companies will use different approaches, based on their circumstances and goals but, in Kanter's words:[7]

> "...despite differences in strategies and tactics, all turnaround leaders share the overarching task of restoring confidence through empowerment – replacing denial with dialogue, blame with respect, isolation with collaboration, and helplessness with opportunities for initiative. Each leader must manage the tricky task of creating a winner's attitude in people, even before the victories."

13.3 GM Today – An Example Turnaround?

It is worth spending a moment discussing GM, as it is the "poster child" for strong and bad cultures that new leadership is trying to change as part of a turnaround. There *are* encouraging signs. GM has an explicit and clear core purpose. There is a new emphasis on accountability and leadership that has been absent for decades. Many outsiders were put in positions of leadership along with GM executives from Asia Pacific and Latin American operations.[8] The new leadership has purged the financial staff's bean-counter mentality that confused cost and value. There is zero tolerance for ethical failures, even when occurring among the most important and visible executives (another necessary change). The overlapping committees have been taken out. All of this is promising.

What we need to see is a revitalized workforce, both white collar and union. Morale has clearly improved from the depths of 2009; people are no longer terrified and in despair. But the cultural transformation still has distance to go. If the company is going to be strong and

---

7   Kanter, op. cit.
8   GM's Asia Pacific and Latin American operations had very different cultures than the North American and Western Europe business units; they were much healthier, almost role models of a good corporate culture. See *Retooling* for more detail.

healthy, the new people and old timers need to form a collage, where they create something new blending the best of both.

The following steps are imperative if GM is to become a healthy company:

- ◆ There must be a strong external focus,
- ◆ A "winner's attitude" and self-respect must be created,
- ◆ Mutual trust must be built across the organization,
- ◆ The attitude toward leadership must shift from fear/reverence to respect, and
- ◆ The leaders recruited from outside and those promoted from within must become one team.

All of these are important and need to happen quickly or GM will not be able to manage the wide range of business problems confronting them. Vehicle markets are becoming more competitive: the Japanese have bounced back from their natural and self-inflicted disasters, the Koreans are quite keen on selling to the world, VW is strong and ambitious to be number one, China is growing rapidly in the background, and climate change could impose new rules. Survival requires all the capabilities of the organization focusing on making the right decisions and meeting these existential threats.

14

Managing Alligators: Making Projects Successful

Sometimes we simply have to survive corporate culture. There is neither the time, nor resources, nor mandate to fix it – only the need to complete our mission. This is especially true for big projects.

Projects differ from normal operations. They have a specific task to perform and there is a distinct beginning, middle, and end (although some seem to go on forever). Participants come from different parts of the company and return when the effort is over. Their time commitments range from minor to all consuming, but there is usually a dedicated core team whose careers depend on the result. Leaders are typically drawn from the mid-level executive ranks and staff from the levels below, although very large projects may be led by someone who reports to the management committee.

Projects are about change. They are magnets for culture's self-preserving mechanisms. They also become flash points for cultural weaknesses: they need an external focus, internal trust, sound leadership, a proper time sense, and hard work. Projects have thin staffing, a fast pace, and senior management attention. These conditions make projects vulnerable to cultural alligators that can be serious obstacles and even fatal problems.

The purpose of this chapter is to summarize tools for anticipating culture-related problems *at the beginning of a project*. This allows the team to plan for them and (sometimes) bypass them altogether. One of our major insights is that different parts of corporate culture *impact projects in distinct ways*. Understanding the specific strengths and weaknesses of a company's culture provides the basis for anticipating and managing problems. Instead of walking into significant problems, teams can step around them.

Very healthy cultures make it hard to fail. The projects can count on good leadership, internal trust, quality debate, sound financials, and so on. On the other hand, very bad cultures will doom projects. Most people work in companies in the "yellow" zone; the culture is basically healthy but there are some serious cultural issues that will confront project teams. Our comments address this situation.

We have to introduce one new idea: the ingredients of project success. There are standard definitions of project management[1] that break down an effort into phases[2] (e.g., begin, design, fulfill …) and more sophisticated ones that break a project into the path of critical events. They are process steps of varying complexity and focus. While important, they do not go to the heart of what makes a project turn out well or fall apart and they are not useful for understanding cultural impacts.

There is a powerful way of looking at projects that borrows from decision analysis: *decision quality*.[3] While there are some different ways of approaching this, the idea is that a good decision is based on:

♦ *Framing* the problem correctly and looking at the right *alternatives*,

♦ Using the right *information* and analyzing the alternatives (*reasoning*) properly,

♦ Using the right *values* for choosing, and

♦ *Implementing* effectively.

The logical steps (above) for finding correct solutions to problems and implementation form the links in a chain. The quality of the discussion determines the strength of the steel in each link of the chain (see Figure 14.1).

Open and constructive dialogue throughout the process is essential. Since projects are about decisions and implementation, the ideas apply directly. Unlike the process definitions, these are the logical steps needed for coming to correct answers. Incorrect or shoddy work in *any* of the above steps can negate the effectiveness (cost, quality, and/or schedule) of the project.

---

1   Nokes, Sebastian. *The Definitive Guide to Project Management*, 2nd Ed. London (Financial Times / Prentice Hall), 2007.

2   Wysocki, Robert K. *Effective Project Management: Traditional, Adaptive, Extreme*, Wiley, 2011.

3   Howard, Ronald. "Foundations of Decision Analysis Revisited," http://www.usc.edu/dept/create/assets/001/50843.pdf Downloaded April 2013. Also in Edward, Ward et al Editors (2007), *Advances in Decision Analysis: From Foundations to Applications*, Cambridge University Press.

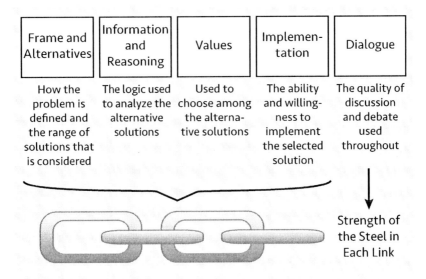

Frame and Alternatives	Information and Reasoning	Values	Implementation	Dialogue
How the problem is defined and the range of solutions that is considered	The logic used to analyze the alternative solutions	Used to choose among the alternative solutions	The ability and willingness to implement the selected solution	The quality of discussion and debate used throughout

Strength of the Steel in Each Link

Figure 14.1: Project Quality Framework

Again, note that a key determinant of project success is the quality of dialogue among the members of the team, the stakeholder organizations, and, not least, between the project and senior management. If a problem is complicated enough to need a dedicated project, it is going to need discussion and debate to manage the complexity and to ensure organizational buy in. Unless these happen, a project will come to a bad end.

14.1 Mapping Culture into Project Quality

Mapping of culture into project quality is shown in Table 14.1. This is a map of the "hot spots" showing where a problem with a cultural trait is likely to show up in a problem with the project.

Two caveats: First, this map should be treated with a bit of caution. We have called out the areas of project quality likely to be affected the most severely, but there could well be other problems, so vigilance is required. Second, this map is generated from a qualitative retrospective of many projects, but project leaders should ask themselves how well it fits with their own experience and organization.

The way to use Table 14.1 is to (1) assess which of the cultural values have the largest gaps in your organization, (2) note which aspects of project quality are likely to be adversely affected by these cultural gaps, and (3) develop a plan at the project staff level to mitigate the

Culture's Impacts on Project Quality			Project Quality				
			Frame and Alternatives	Information and Reasoning	Values	Implementation	Dialogue
C u l t u r a l V a l u e s		0. Core Purpose	↑			↑	
	External Focus	1. External Focus	↑	↑			
	Internal Trust	2. Internal Trust		↑		↑	↑
	Role and Qualifications of Leadership	3. Merit and Accountability	↑			↑	↑
		4. Debate, Dissent, and Discipline	↑	↑		↑	↑
		5. Empowered	↑			↑	↑
		6. Decisions Where They Belong	↑	↑		↑	
	Time Orientation	7. Forward Looking	↑		↑		
		8. Frugality and Investment	↑	↑			
		9. Innovation	↑	↑			
	Basics	10. Strong Work Ethic		↑		↑	
		11. Ethics	↑		↑		↑
		12. Continuous Learning			↑	↑	
		13. Ability Matters Most	↑	↑			

Table 14.1: *Culture's Impacts on Project Quality*

potential adverse effects. The value of this map is it helps project leaders plan for problems. Given an assessment of their company's culture, it shows what cultural challenges the project is likely to face. We also include suggestions for managing these problems. Together, these help project leaders develop a better game plan before the effort begins.

Core Purpose

Loss of Core Purpose creates confusion in a business as there is no "North Star." Project leaders will define problems too broadly and consider too many solutions. Unless the core purpose is clearly stated within the frame of the problem, an effort should confine itself to alternatives consistent with the company's reason for being. But when the core purpose has been weakened, people are uncertain about their boundaries. This can cause loss of efficiency as scarce project resources are spread thinly. It can also lead to wasted effort if the top leaders reject the solution as inappropriate.

A more serious problem is when the project team recommends a solution that the company accepts but cannot do. Most processes and systems are tailored to the specifics of a business. IT, human resources, financial reporting and analysis, and planning systems that work for one business seldom fit another. To the extent a recommendation differs from the existing core purpose, it will be out of alignment with these. The result is a recommendation that cannot be executed or one that costs far more than anticipated. Another problem is that the people responsible for the implementation will get the details wrong, as they are working in unfamiliar territory. A third problem is that a recommendation that is misaligned with the core purpose is likely to meet a great deal of resistance. This is often "passive aggressive," as people do not want to openly fight but they feel strongly that it is wrong. The result is project failure despite much effort.

Since people lack effective guidance, they will be more likely to send the problem to their bosses for resolution. The top levels of the organization are flooded with problems that lower levels should solve and the project teams will lose autonomy and empowerment.

External Focus

An inward-focused company will not see a problem correctly, at least those parts having to do with issues outside their company. Insular companies frame problems as a search for blame, usually blaming external forces such as customers, competitors, or government. Solutions often take the form of speaking louder to convince these entities of their errors, or solutions focus on reorganization or cost control, rather than how to win in the marketplace. Consequently, the project team will neither understand the problem correctly nor look at correct solutions. As they try to analyze the possible alternatives, they will miss important information about customers and others, such as government, and therefore will do a poor job of analysis.

Internal Trust

If there is poor internal trust, information will not flow properly, and what does flow will be viewed with suspicion. Analysis can be hamstrung by incomplete and inaccurate information, leading to poor inputs into models. It is impossible to have real dialogue in an atmosphere of distrust, so meaningful debate never happens. Instead, conflict is hidden and people pretend to agree but do not act. Even if a decision does get made, if it falls outside the normal business processes, implementation can fail due to distrust. Implementation requires improving solutions together, which is hampered by mutual suspicion.

Merit and Accountability

When leaders are not chosen by merit and there is a lack of accountability, it will show up in the frame and alternatives, as well as dialogue and implementation. In these corporate cultures, leaders belong to "the club" and work to stay there. They will drive safe alternatives and standard frames and be will reluctant to cause turbulence. As a consequence, people will be averse to vigorous debate. Lack of accountability will lead to bold sounding alternatives but they will be all vision and never budgeted. People will be comforted but not threatened. Implementation will be haphazard, as people are not held accountable for final results and only the safest recommendations will actually happen. The quality of the discussion is poor, as people avoid surfacing issues that could be embarrassing or that they would be responsible for managing.

Debate, Dissent, and Discipline

When debate and dissent are weak, the senior person in the room sets the frame and the alternatives. If these are weak, then the solution will be weak as well. At the least, alternatives miss the sharpening that comes from vigorous discussion. Fallacies and foolishness live on and find their way into the project. Alternatives are likely to be safe ones that do not challenge the established direction. The reasoning is likely to be poor if the problem is complex, as complex problems require strong debate and discussion. And, of course, dialogue is poor without debate and dissent.

People often engage in delaying or diversionary tactics to avoid action. A popular tactic is to call for more information, research, or data. As a consequence, the lack of debate and dissent results in fewer decisions being made. Lack of discipline means that people will not feel any need to obey a decision with which they disagree. Therefore implementation does not happen unless there is universal consensus.

Empowered

Lack of empowerment leads to a frame and alternatives that are too mild and close to the status quo. People will not feel comfortable with strong solutions that need change. Team members will look at one another and complain there is nothing they can do about the "system," so they will not try. Arguing with authority is simply not done, so the dialogue will be weak. Since implementation requires making many decisions quickly and occasionally upsetting people, implementation is delayed as people delay making the decisions or avoid them altogether.

Decisions Where They Belong

Because the team is far away from the problem, they are unlikely to understand it properly or look at the right set of solutions. Alternatives are unrealistic. Risks are poorly understood. Information is incomplete, misleading, or incorrect. Solutions cannot be implemented as they fail to account for important issues. Dialogue is hampered by distance, not ill will or lack of ability. Because the team is not empowered with the correct level of decision-making authority, they spend much time providing information to far-away management, so cost and schedule commitments are unlikely to be achieved.

Forward Looking

When people are oriented to the past, they will define the problem in terms of how to get back to the past. Alternatives will be crafted to recreate the lost "glory" days, sometimes by asking, "What would the founder do?" Choices will be reactionary. The values brought to bear on the problem will be how well it recreates the past, not how well it defines the future.

Frugality and Investment

When frugality is lost, alternatives are unbounded by constraints and costs are missing from the analysis. However, if the importance of investment is lost, cost control rules the day, to the detriment of the product and sometimes to the safety and lives of employees. In either case, the frame and alternatives are wrong. The analysis of the alternatives is deeply flawed as well because one side of the "Revenue – Costs = Profits" equation is wrong.

Innovation

Teams stick to the tried and true because they do not see the value in experimenting or trying something new. They underestimate the value of innovation, often discounting innovative alternatives heavily in the cash flows – after all, it is not "proven." Alternatives that are about exploring possibilities and creating option value are not considered. Discount rates are often too high.

Strong Work Ethic

Implementation is hard work, and this falls apart in projects when people are averse to the hard work necessary to make something happen. Analysis requires tedious work: gathering data, ensuring its validity, and coding complex models. If this is not done rigorously, the analysis is poor. People work on presentations to management but do not do the work required to make it of high quality.

Ethics

Poor ethics leads to losing sight of improving the business. The focus shifts to a self-serving frame and alternatives. It can lead to outright bending the analysis or corrupting it completely. *High quality analysis requires honesty*. Poor ethics hinders honest debate.

Continuous Learning

A lack of continuous learning leads to people being out of touch with recent changes in technology, markets, and society. Without continuous learning, people are five to ten years behind, if not more. There is poor understanding of issues that would be commonplace in more current environments. The results are poorly framed problems and poor quality analysis.

Ability Matters Most

When background is valued over ability, the result is that only certain voices are heard. As a practical matter, women, minorities, gays, the young, and the "different" are not listened to (if they are present at all). The result is a narrow worldview that is likely to miss important issues. This leads to poor understanding of the problem and alternatives too close to the status quo.

14.2 Creating Alligator Management Plans

Strong project leaders can do a great deal to avoid these alligators, if they are aware of them and engage in some planning. We make recommendations for coping with the problems, not solving the underlying malady. As we said in the introduction to this section, this chapter is designed to help projects survive the challenges from cultural issues and accomplish their mission successfully.

We list some suggested tips in Table 14.2. Most have been discussed in earlier chapters in the sections describing remedies available to managers, so we avoid repetition.

14.3 Example: Product Development Strategy

The following is an example of how understanding possible cultural challenges within a company can contribute to the success of a project.

John Bigelow, General Director of Manufacturing for North America at Global Electronics, and Peter Oswald, General Director of Marketing for North America, had been asked by top management to develop a new product strategy for a major set of products. They were made co-leaders of a cross-functional team of ten people who were committed to the effort for half to full time for three months. The decision board included four vice presidents and the President of North America. The CEO sanctioned the project and was eagerly awaiting its recommendations.

Both John and Peter had some concerns about the company's culture and decided to do a one-day workshop with their team. They asked an outsider to help facilitate the effort as they wanted a neutral but strong voice who could guide them through the workshop.

The leaders were familiar with *Creating a Culture of Profitability*, but the rest of team was not, so the workshop began with a presentation of the model of culture. After some lively discussion, the participants felt comfortable enough to advance to the first step: an assessment of their company's culture. At first, there was discomfort talking about cultural problems, but they were assured that everything said in the room would stay in the room. The team was also promised the work would be used only

Cultural Value	Alligator Management Tips
0. Core Purpose	Keep frame aligned with core purpose Include implementation issues in frame Surface lack of alignment with review board Implementation plan must address all of the issues
1. External Focus	Experiential learning Primary research Benchmarking Outside speakers Outside help Extra care with influence diagram Listening
2. Internal Trust	Commit to change Strong facilitation Trust building through work (meet face-to-face) Use "back doors" to get required data Use "work arounds" to get decision quality Surface barriers with review board Ask RB to appoint a "guerrilla" Create dedicated team
3. Merit and Accountability	Do the work; give the boss the credit Find talent and try to ally / bring on board Try to get good leaders to take over; oversee Exert control over review board membership Use good leaders to overcome bad ones Use "work arounds" to get project quality
4. Debate, Dissent, and Discipline	Strong facilitation Debate but extra politely Use individual discussion for debate, not group meetings (shuttle diplomacy) Use better leaders as counter-balance to bad ones Use extra care on analysis, more detail and rigor Distribute analysis widely, especially to review board Insist on data If someone says earth is flat, find someone sane at review board level who can counter Do work outside organization Consider elimination of PowerPoint
5. Empowered	Self-empower (Just do it) Strong facilitation (give backbone) Extra dialogue Pick team of hard chargers Count on doing more of the work yourself Outsource

Table 14.2: Alligator Management Tips (Part 1)

Cultural Value	Alligator Management Tips
6. Decisions Where They Belong	Locate project properly Have review board members who are near problem Have core team members on project from right location If cannot locate properly, interview/include as many as possible who are near the problem May need to do extensive phone conferencing and interviews plus bend sleep cycle Extra effort to include local information in analysis Consider proxy advisory board of local leaders Move analysis team to right location
7. Forward Looking	Bring in "adults" Formal decision processes Expose to ideas Experiential learning Surface issue of discount rate and keep in reasonable range "Visionary" and "Reactionary" strategies should both be viewed with suspicion Discuss relevance of history explicitly Include "intangibles" in analysis Use internal or external lessons for "benchmark" behavior
8. Frugality and Investment	Balance the tendency to overestimate costs or ignore them Formal dialogue with review board to surface issue Facilitation and analysis support
9. Innovation	Force innovation into alternatives Use outsiders to help establish need or act as source Look at world leaders to understand what they are doing and showcase problems If discount rate is too high (>10%), debate at review board Surface rules and financial requirements that hinder innovation and discuss with review board
10. Strong Work Ethic 11. Ethics 12. Continuous Learning 13. Ability Matters Most	Outsource if necessary Do the work yourself Cherry pick team of hard workers or find pockets of talent Surface issue with review board In framing stage, dedicate portion of the project to looking broadly at issues (especially long-term issues) Keep it simple

Table 14.2: Alligator Management Tips (Part 2)

to ensure the success of the project; this was not about how to transform the company.

With those issues put to rest, the team continued to the assessment. They were comfortable with using a qualitative scale of

Area	Healthy	Unhealthy	Assess-ment
Respect for Outside World	Believe respect must always be won anew	Sense of entitlement combined with condescension	**Good**
Products Hit Their Target	Well-designed products and services that meet customer needs, occasionally inspired design	Mediocre products that often miss and seldom delight	**Good**
Sense and Manage External Forces	See external trends and forces and can manage them	Deaf to important external forces and miss important threats and opportunities	**OK**
See Need to Change	Willing to change as external circumstances change	Stick to the status quo for too long	**Poor**
Relationship with External Stakeholders	Play well with others	Poor record of working with allies, suppliers, distributors	**Good**
Reaction to External Critics	Mindful listening to external critics	Respond defensively to criticism by saying they are misunderstood and under-appreciated	**Good**
Role of Government	Provide level playing field Seek solutions in the marketplace	Seek legislative and regulatory remedies to market problems	**Good**
Lifestyles	Diverse set of lifestyles	Leaders live in same neighborhoods, go to same clubs, churches, etc.	**Good**

Table 14.3: Team Self-assessment of External Focus Symptoms

Good/OK/Poor for each of the cultural traits (with poor being considered an "alligator"). They went down the list one by one and, with one exception, could agree on each of the traits. The exception was the question of external focus, where the team seemed unable to come to agreement. To help clarify the discussion, they went to the table of symptoms and evaluated each of them on the Good/OK/Poor scale (see Table 14.3, which is similar to Figure 6.1 except it includes the team's assessments).

The team realized that they had a problem with sensing external forces and saw a need for a change, but in the other areas the company was healthy. They decided to allocate effort for scanning external trends and to be vigilant for conservative forces that were resistant to necessary change.

The team reached agreement on external focus and they were able to complete the map (see Table 14.4).

The team found this map insightful and helpful. It was consistent with their intuition but gave them a strong detailed grasp of their organization. It also catalyzed putting plans in place at the beginning of the project. Below is part of their plan:

♦ Innovation alligators
  • Extra effort to look at innovation opportunities
  • Look outside, or to different sources, for ideas
  • Surface financial rules that hinder innovation
♦ Decisions-where-they-belong alligators
  • Move the project team to the right location
  • Shift decision makers and delegation of authority
  • Local intelligence gathering responsibilities assigned
♦ Core Purpose cautions
  • Watch for drift to cool sounding alternatives that are outside scope of enterprise
♦ Internal Trust cautions
  • Build direct relationships with information sources, internal partners, implementers at the beginning of the project
♦ Ability cautions
  • Worry about mediocre people on team
  • Exert extra control on staff

In addition, the number of cautions on implementation suggested thought be given to the organization's ability to deliver as they developed their strategy and including "tactical" issues in the main part of the effort, rather than deferring them.

The company went on to have a successful project. The team kept their assessment of the possible cultural challenges strictly to themselves as they carried out their work, but after the project was completed they held a special discussion with the decision

Team's Cultural Issue / Project Roadmap	Assessment	Frame and Alternatives	Information and Reasoning	Values	Implementation	Dialogue
0. Core Purpose	OK	OK			OK	
1. External Focus	Good	G	G			
2. Internal Trust	OK		OK		OK	OK
3. Merit and Accountability	Good	G			G	G
4. Debate, Dissent, and Discipline	Good	G	G			G
5. Empowered	OK	OK				OK
6. Decisions Where They Belong	Poor	P	P		P	P
7. Forward Looking	Good	G		G		
8. Frugality and Investment	Good	G	G			
9. Innovation	Poor	P	P			
10. Strong Work Ethic	Good		G		G	
11. Ethics	Good	G		G		G
12. Continuous Learning	OK		OK	OK		
13. Ability Matters Most	Good	G	G			

Table 14.4: Team Project Road Map

board on their cultural observations. This led to a discussion with the CEO, who decided to increase the emphasis on innovation and to make sure that decisions were properly placed. He also agreed to an overall review of the company's corporate structure.

14.4 Applicability

There are five groups who should be concerned about potential cultural problems affecting major projects:

♦ Project leaders and their teams. While preferably done at the beginning of a project, this assessment can also be effective later if the team faces unexpectedly severe cultural problems and needs to regroup to manage them.

- Internal consulting activities responsible for managing large projects. This perspective will give them the tools for running these efforts more effectively. These groups should also be "eyes and ears" for senior management for cultural problems. They will see the problems and looking across projects will alert them to a systemic problem. These activities can serve as a cultural "radar."

- Joint venture projects. These teams need to manage multiple cultures and develop an understanding of one another. Alliances are always problematic but are becoming more common, especially in capital-intensive industries.

- Organization Development (OD) departments and professionals who are on the front lines of managing cultural issues. They will gain a deeper understanding of corporate culture and how to manage it.

- Senior Leadership, especially those overseeing multiple projects. They must understand how to make multiple efforts more effective and where the key issues live within their company's culture.

If a company uses a stage gate or phase gate process to manage major projects, the best time to assess culture is at the beginning of each project phase. This is because the focus of the work and the people working on the project are likely to change during the transition between phases of the project. As phases change, it is especially important to consider relationships with key stakeholders (e.g., the engineering design firm, permitting agencies, labor unions, etc.).

15

Culture and Profitability: A Test

The premise of this book is that the right culture is a necessary condition for lasting profitability. The cultural model is strongly supported by data from nations, including surveys, case studies, and longitudinal studies. However, these models focus on countries, not companies. Ideas should be tested and we are about to present some data, cautiously, supporting our claim.

Our case for a culture of profitability is reasonable and many authors have argued for parts of our cultural recommendations for a long time, from sound ethics to a clear purpose. And no one has argued companies should not have these qualities. Few suggest enterprises turn a blind eye to the external world, view their colleagues with suspicion, pick bad leaders, let them do as they would, disregard the future, spurn innovation, keep women and minorities down, ignore continuing training and education, and treat ethics as silly impediments to action. Although some might find it attractive to be a boss in such a company, the problem is the likely short term of employment, perhaps followed by time spent as an incarcerated guest of the state.

In constructing our test, we worked to overcome two common mistakes: sample selection bias and the halo effect. We needed reliable data corresponding to our definition of corporate culture, while making sure we understood other possible measures and why they were not used.

The most important objective of this test is to be clear about what we did, why we did it, and the choices we made about our data and methods. This transparency helps ensure we are using the data that make the most sense and provide the most rigorous test, not the most favorable.

Our claims are different from the claims of most business books. Our claim: our model of culture lets business leaders manage culture in the same way they manage issues such as costs and customers. Our point is that culture is a necessary condition for profitability, but not close to being a sufficient one. *There is no formula for success and we are not offering one.* On the contrary, success can be very difficult, short-lived, and subject to setbacks and near-death experiences. Lasting profitability means managing complexity in a turbulent and sometimes hostile environment. We hope to add to the business leader's arsenal, but the arsenal needs to be a well-stocked room.

There should be a reasonable degree of confidence this weapon is worth having, that it is not loaded with blanks or, worse, would backfire. An optimal test would be to develop reliable measures of the cultural qualities, apply them to a random sample of companies, and follow them over time. Even if this were possible, the best we could do is to disprove the theory. This is because good culture is needed but is not always enough. So if a company had a good culture but failed, it could be due to any number of other issues (the operation was a success but the patient died).

We are willing to assert there are no cases of lasting success with a "bad" culture in the sense we defined it, unless the company is in a protected economy, such as China or Russia. One of the strengths of our argument is that the reader can test this proposition against his or her own experience.

Please note many successful companies have cultures that we find personally unpleasant, but that is not the point. The specifics of a good culture have little to do with traits we find personally congenial. If a company can be arrogant while keeping an external perspective and allowing internal debate and dissent, there is nothing wrong with arrogance. If you are going to design, build, and run a billion dollar oil platform in deep and violent seas, self-confidence is probably a valuable quality.

15.1 Sample Selection Bias and Halo Effect

To test our theory, we need to address problems plaguing other empirical work. One serious problem is sample selection bias. A study of why companies succeed or fail must look at companies doing both, not just successful companies. *This is a crippling error, not a minor quibble.* It is impossible to understand success unless you can tell how it differs from failure. The other serious data problem is the "halo effect," where data are contaminated because of subjective judgments.

The world is full or reasonable theories that turned out to be wrong, especially in business.[1] The business literature is bursting with examples of how companies once considered great failed. *In Search of Excellence,* a phenomenal best seller written 30 years ago, described many companies as "excellent" that ended up failing.

Two other influential books, *Built to Last*[2] and *Good to Great,*[3] were both written by Jim Collins. Several companies noted in these books followed a similar fate. As Phil Rosensweig has pointed out,[4] these studies suffer from two major problems:

♦ Sample selection bias in Peters' work, where they only looked at successful companies, and

♦ Data bias in Collins work.

In this latter case, the problem is that most of the "data" on qualities such as a company's leadership, strategy, culture and so on come from opinion surveys of business people and/or journalists. These opinions are hopelessly confounded by the overall financial success of the company – a company making money rates high on everything and vice versa. This is the "Halo Effect," a well-known problem in consumer product evaluations.

Collins defends himself in a new book, *How the Mighty Fall,*[5] shielding his earlier claims on the grounds that success breeds a fatal disease. This does not mean there is anything wrong with his prescription for health; we have also argued that success can be its own enemy. And he may be correct – at the least all the ideas in these books are sensible and none are at odds with my arguments about the importance of culture. But many ideas in the literature become orthodoxy without much evidence, often to the serious harm of good business and clear thinking.[6]

---

1   Pfeffer, Jeffrey and Sutton, Robert (2006) *Hard Facts, Dangerous Half-Truths And Total Nonsense: Profiting From Evidence-Based Management,* Harvard Business School Press.

2   Collins, Jim and Jerry I. Porras, (1994) *Built to Last: Successful Habits of Visionary Companies,* Harper Business.

3   Collins, Jim (2001) *Good to Great: Why Some Companies Make the Leap ... and Others Don't,* Random House Business Books.

4   Rosenzweig, Phil. (2007) "The Halo Effect: Misunderstanding the Halo Effect and Other Business Delusions," California Management Review.

5   Collins, Jim. (2009) *How the Mighty Fall: And Why Some Companies Never Give In,* Jim Collins.

6   Pfeffer, op. cit.

15.2 Objective Data and Avoiding the Halo

It is important to test these ideas and we have done so. Despite the earlier comments, *we would expect companies with excellent cultures to do better than their competitors*. We should be skeptical of these ideas if the data showed otherwise. To see if this is the case, we looked for data on companies that would give us an indication of the culture. One requirement we imposed is that the data be publicly available. There are two reasons:

♦ Publicly available data released by companies must be vetted for accuracy, thanks to Sarbanes Oxley and its EU equivalents.

♦ We wanted to test our model of culture as an investment strategy, which meant limiting our information to "non-secret" stuff.

A better culture should translate into a higher shareholder return and that is the metric we used.

We examined several sources of data. The two sources that best measure culture are the Fortune/CNN Poll of Top 100 Places to Work and Corporate Responsibility (CR) Magazine's Top 100. The measure of cultural quality we used was the total number of mentions for each preceding year in either category, using data from 2005 through 2012, and taking the top 25 as our test portfolio.

Fortune/CNN developed their rankings through employee surveys and a cultural audit, filled out by the company and administered by the Great Place to Work Institute. Companies had to be at least five years old with at least 1000 employees. If news about the company damaged the Institute's faith in the company, the company was dropped. Their measures focus on trust, pride, and respect. These correlate well with leadership picked on merit, accountability, toleration of debate and dissent, and decentralized decision making. It also suggests being forward looking, having a proper time sense, and ethical behavior. An organization with high degrees of internal distrust would score poorly on this assessment. More important, we think a good culture is a "happy" culture, so assessments of employees should reflect this. These data are subject to the bias of Rosenzweig's halo effect, but much less so than data from outsiders and analysts, as these data are from insiders with firsthand experience. Still, employees' evaluation of their work environment could be swayed by the size of their paycheck and financial success of their employer. It is well documented, however, that even workers at low paying companies, such as Starbucks, are willing to rate their conditions favorably.

The other source we used was CR (Corporate Responsibility) Magazine Top 100. This is a little less intuitive than using data on the quality of the work life, which has a more direct link with a company's culture. A close look at their methodology shows why this metric is a good indicator of culture. The measure emphasizes disclosure and transparency across a broad range of metrics. In 2012, there were 318 measures across seven categories, all publicly available. We have worked in sustainability for some time and noticed two phenomena:

♦ Companies comfortable disclosing data are usually well connected to the world around them (not insular).

♦ Successful companies are usually comfortable with accountability, even when things are not going well.

Granted, these metrics are subjective, but they are based on experience.

Disclosing the large amounts of data required to make the CR Top 100 means the organization needs to be relatively seamless. In a company with many silos, the information will not flow to those inside the company responsible for collecting it (typically central staffers). The operating units where much of the data reside will ignore the data requests, which are of little immediate value to those providing it. Another advantage of the CR Top 100 is that all the companies within the Russell 1000 are evaluated, so there is no sample selection bias. The analysis is mostly rule based, with some intervention to account for news that might result in a company being ineligible.

We also looked at several other measures of sustainability, including the Dow Jones Sustainability Index (DJSI), the FTSE4Good Index, the Newsweek Green Rankings, and the Global 100. All these performed worse than market averages. Figure 15.1 compares the Dow Jones Sustainability Index with the S&P 500.

Over the last one, five, and ten years, the "sustainable" stocks have not outperformed the market. (The FTSE4Good index performs about the same as the DJSI.)

There are three reasons the DJSI underperforms the market.

♦ First, companies self-select to take part, unlike for the CR Top 100, where every company is evaluated. Anytime there is self-selection in a study, the results are in question as motivations are unclear. It could be the companies

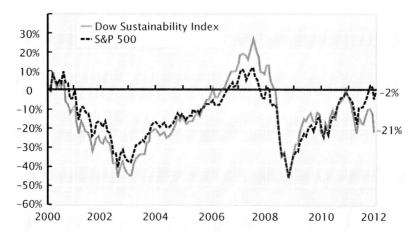

Figure 15.1: Dow Jones Sustainability Index and S&P 500

> who choose to join are the ones not doing as well as their
> peers and are looking for some "edge" or public relations
> benefit.
>
> ♦ Second, the measures are vaguely defined.
>
> ♦ Third, the data are based on surveys filled out by the com-
> panies, not publicly available data. The index's authors
> claim this allows greater depth in the analysis, but the
> real effect is to cast doubt on the truth of the data; they
> are not verifiable in any way.

We looked at several other indices and all underperformed the market.
One was the Newsweek Green Rankings, based heavily on environmental impact assessed by an independent party. Reasonable as a
measure of "green," this has little to do with our definition of a good
culture. So it is no surprise Newsweek's Green Rankings have little, or
negative, correlation with performance. The Corporate Knights rankings, published by Forbes, are a confused mix of variables indicating
"clean capitalism," but the measures are not transparent and rely on
information provided by companies, so it is no surprise that there is
little correlation to culture or shareholder return. Like the Newsweek
rankings, they significantly underperform the market.

Name	Performance		Top 25 Culture Companies			
	52 Week	5 Year	2012	2011	2010	2009
Accenture	28.8%	57.4%	x	x		
Adobe	49.0%	-16.2%	x	x	x	x
Aflac	33.3%	-13.2%	x	x	x	x
Applied Materials Inc.	10.9%	-42.3%	x	x	x	x
Cisco	26.4%	-36.4%	x	x	x	x
General Mills	7.5%	38.0%	x	x	x	x
Google	37.9%	35.4%	x	x	x	x
Gap	129.4%	108.4%	x	x	x	x
Goldman Sachs	-7.3%	-40.8%	x	x	x	x
Intel	37.2%	11.1%	x	x	x	x
Intuit	36.9%	108.6%	x	x	x	x
Nordstrom	52.9%	21.8%	x	x	x	x
CarMax	17.6%	34.4%	x	x	x	x
Marriott International	53.8%	-9.1%	x	x	x	x
Mattel	51.0%	56.5%	x	x	x	x
Microsoft	28.5%	9.4%	x	x	x	x
National Instruments	18.6%	27.2%	x	x	x	x
Nike Inc. (Cl B)	22.5%	76.7%	x	x	x	x
NetApp	-6.9%	28.8%	x	x	x	x
PepsiCo	18.2%	5.8%	x	x	x	x
Qualcomm	36.0%	68.6%	x	x	x	x
Starbucks	37.4%	80.6%	x	x	x	x
State Street Corp.	31.3%	-34.5%	x	x	x	x
Texas Instruments Inc.	20.3%	-9.8%	x	x	x	x
Whole Foods Market	68.4%	116.1%	x	x	x	x
Portfolio Return	**33.6%**	**27.3%**				
Index ETF						
SPY (S&P 500)	26.2%	-1.7%				
DIA (Dow)	22.7%	1.4%				
ONEQ (NASDAQ)	22.4%	23.4%				
IWB(RUSSEL 1000)	25.7%	0.1%				

Table 15.1: Top 25 "Culture Companies" Performance

15.3 Results

Table 15.1 shows the Top 25 "Culture Companies" for 2009-2012 (prior to 2009, there were not enough data to pick the top 25) and their performance over the last year and for five years (as of August 2012). These companies significantly outperformed the market in both the short and long term.

Note that the cultural assessment of these stocks was stable, an important finding to support the analysis. This is what we would expect for cultural measures, as the underlying culture changes slowly. Also, the combined measure outperformed each one taken separately.

15.4 Caveats

There are some reasons to be cautious about our results, as promising as they are. The biggest problem is we do not use true "out of sample" tests. While the 2012 performance was based on 2011 data, developing the metric was based on the last five years or so of data and comparing the performance of different metrics. While we did not manipulate the data and are comfortable we were as rigorous as possible, the concern remains. A source of comfort is that the reasons for the performance of the metrics are clear – this is not an exercise in curve fitting. But, in the jargon of all those prospectuses, current performance does not guarantee future performance.

A second concern is the measure misses innovation, at least directly. We tried to use the Forbes Innovation Ranking, but this is problematic. The measure looks at price over the discounted cash flow of expected earnings and calls the difference an "Innovation Premium." This premium could be anything; it is simply an unexplained high stock price. It directly selects for companies with a surprisingly high stock price and is not, as the authors carefully and clearly state, a good indicator of future performance. The Bloomberg Business Week Innovation index is another publicly available index. It is based on a survey of outsiders, making it prone to Halo problems and growth rates in earnings and margins. It also failed to outperform the market during the time period we examined.

A third problem is the exclusion of companies with good cultures but in industries that are almost automatically dismissed, especially energy, chemicals, and mining. We are familiar with Chevron – they pride themselves on their culture and, in our opinion, rightly so. Because Toyota and Honda are Japanese companies, they were not included, however, we think their cultures are among the world's best.

15.5 Conclusion

We conclude that these results support our arguments on culture and its economic value. In the spirit of putting our money where our mouth is, and for full disclosure, we have moved a substantial portion of our equity portfolio into these stocks. But these results call out for a research effort for companies similar to the one in scope and scale that Lawrence Harrison and his colleagues carried out for nations.

16

Culture as a Limit to Growth

Our ideas on the role of culture and profitability have strong implications about lasting growth and success: if a company wants to continue to grow, it must manage its culture.

We have argued that success and growth erode the cultural traits needed for profitability. Senior leadership becomes more distant from the external world and can lose direct and visceral connection with customers. As organizations grow, the distances between people widen to make fellow employees strangers to one another; distrust and silos follow. Complex incentive systems are impossible to align and drive the wrong behavior, stimulating internal competition. The gap between decisions and outcomes makes it difficult to preserve accountability and merit becomes hard to determine. Niceness and collegiality become more important than excellence as lifetime employment becomes a reality (this is discussed further in Appendix IV).

Table 16.1 summarizes the forces of entropy from the previous chapters. The forces that are part of success and growth are highlighted. As the table shows, many of the issues that cause cultural decay are part and parcel of success and growth.

Profitability becomes its own enemy and, after a certain point, growth stalls and decline follows. Without active management, natural forces erode the values needed for success. None of this is inevitable, it just needs active management. Company cost structures also have similar issues: success breeds a lack of discipline and an eroding position. Customers must always be won anew. Realizing this, successful companies manage these issues aggressively.

Yet culture is not managed (parts and pieces, perhaps, but not in its entirety nor to the degree necessary). Successful companies feeling growing pains need to pay the closest attention, as do former superstars

Core Purpose	Market forces
	Founder replaced by professional managers who lack the passion and commitment
	New recruits attracted for financial reasons, not commitment
	Human Resources puts in measurement systems that focus only on functional abilities
External Focus	Fear of the marketplace
	Large size means distance from customer
	Specialized staffs (e.g. Marketing, Government Relations) control access to the outside world
	Capital efficiency demands from Wall Street push towards franchise models
	Antitrust threats when too successful
Internal Trust	Human nature
	Pockets of incompetence
	Size of company causes silos
	Organizational complexity causes disconnects between parts
	Misaligned compensation systems
Leadership	People flee accountability
	Growth creates gap between decisons and results
	Emphasis on niceness rather than holding people accountable
Time Orientation	Childish: Unexamined victories are seen as inevitable
	Aged: Long period of success leads to insularity and silos, resulting in inability to change
Basics	As it was in the beginning …
	Values of society surrounding firm

Table 16.1: Summary, Forces of Entropy
          (shaded areas result from growth and success)

who have stalled out. Culture now becomes the important "limiting reagent" on growth. People understand the effects of cost and customers on growth, but the understanding of culture is very limited.

17

Public Policy and Corporate Culture

The discussion so far has focused on how a company can manage its own culture, but there is a need to understand the role of public policy in fostering a culture of profitability. As companies manage their corporate culture, they should also think about how to affect public policies that reinforce good corporate culture.

These ideas are relevant for companies operating in the BRICs (Brazil, Russia, India, China) and other emerging national economies. In these nations, domestic and multi-national companies play important roles. The local leaders of multinationals often have a great deal of influence on the governments where they operate. The local business leadership socializes at the highest levels (much more so than in the US or Europe). Most Asian societies enjoy a strong tradition of public/private cooperation, especially China, Japan, Korea, Singapore, and Taiwan. In these countries it will be quite natural to think about how the public sector can help the private sector be stronger.

Most nations want to create a vibrant private sector and governments are often shareholders in private enterprise. Private sector profitability and public prosperity go together, each driving the other. The core cultural traits for profitability in the private sector are closely related to the broader culture that leads to prosperity and freedom in society. Government policy therefore has an impact beyond helping the private sector thrive. It reinforces the overall movement toward a democratic and flourishing nation. As Douglass North said, "Societies that get 'stuck' embody belief systems and institutions that fail to confront and solve new problems of societal complexity."[1]

Government has a role in influencing the culture of business. Government wields powerful levers, including the establishment of laws and regulations, control of the tax code, its buying power, its media access to influence opinion, and its power to establish role models.

The basics are the easiest parts of culture that government can affect because laws and regulations can target them directly. Ethical codes are the easiest to legislate, although even developed nations exhibit problems fighting corruption. Strongly enforced laws reinforce a company's internal ethical codes. Legislation can increase the value of women and minorities in the workplace, as many societies have done.[2] Education can be incentivized through tax subsidies; government can set up educational programs and spread information directly. In the United States, community colleges are a good example, as are the state-run Cooperative Extension Services. Government influence on the work ethic is more problematic, although it can ensure fair competition and prevent labor practices such as featherbedding.

Time orientation can be shaped by tax policy on consumption and savings, the stability of regulatory environment, and the rule of law. Much research shows the importance of government creating a climate that encourages economic success, ranging from anti-corruption campaigns to expedited licensing procedures. Innovation is an area where public policy can have a major impact through the educational system, universities and technical institutes, government sponsorship of research through grants and contracts, immigration policies, intellectual property laws, and the tax code. India and China are good examples of how public policy affects innovation, as is Israel.[3]

Public policy's influence on *leadership* can be direct in enterprises where the state has some ownership interest and can exert its influence at the board level to drive a healthy culture of leadership. Because

1   North, Douglass. (1993) "Economic Performance Through Time," Persson, Torsten ed. (1997) Nobel Lectures, Economics 1991-1995, World Scientific Publishing Co. Also at http://nobelprize.org/nobel_prizes/economics/laureates/1993/north-lecture.html.

2   Beate Gordon slipped women's equality into the Japanese constitution created right after WW2, with a profound impact on that society. http://www.nytimes.com/2013/01/02/world/asia/beate-gordon-feminist-heroine-in-japan-dies-at-89.html?ref=obituaries&_r=0.

3   Senor, Dan and Singer, Saul, op. cit.

leadership roles and qualifications are set at the top and driven down, this may be an effective avenue of government influence. The success of well-led companies would then reinforce selecting competent leaders in businesses where government had a less direct interest. Another way government can develop the right business leaders is through the institutions producing them. In many countries, government plays an important role in the leading national business schools and can ensure the right values are instilled in its future leaders. Israel is an interesting case where the military had an important role in training leaders for high tech businesses and creating a culture of innovation.[4]

Internal trust and external identification are more difficult to influence through public policy, but are still important. The government has many ways to affect corporate culture. It can use media to publicize companies that are role models. It can engage in public relations initiatives, such as a campaign for gender equality or ongoing education. Political leaders can ask respected business leaders to carry the message to other CEOs. Government can conduct studies on successful business practices and spread the results in the private sector.

Most companies focus their public policy efforts on items of immediate economic interest: usually tax incentives, supportive regulations, and anti-corruption measures. But they should consider shifting some portion of their effort to issues that create a durable climate for profitability.

---

4   Senor, Dan and Singer, Saul, op. cit.

18
Conclusion

Business leaders no longer have an excuse to roll their eyes when someone talks about corporate culture. If leaders have the will, we have provided the way for them to manage culture with the same rigor as any other major business driver. There is neither a magic formula, nor a panacea, nor a promise that managing culture is *the* secret to success. It is one of the important areas of management that can now be handled.

We have developed a conceptual model that is detailed enough to be useful and that is based on data and is testable against experience. There is no reason to take the ideas on faith; they should resonate with experience. There are detailed symptoms and metrics for each of the cultural ills that show leadership where the problems lie before they become overpowering. We have suggested reasonable and doable treatment plans that attack the symptoms and root causes; undoubtedly people will find others and improve upon them. There is a workable way to start integrating cultural management into the existing organization without adding bureaucracy or overhead.

Culture matters. Everyone knows that. But now you can do something about it.

Appendix I:
Lawrence Harrison's Culture Matters Research Project and Trait Typology of High Cultural Capital and Low Cultural Capital Societies

The founding father of modern research on culture and its role in the development of nations is Lawrence Harrison. He catalyzed much of the research done over the last 25 years. He pulled together a broad group of academics, journalists, and government officials, created a vibrant intellectual community among them. He shaped, focused, and supported their research as well as his own. Harrison's first volume was a collection of essays from some of the world's leading thinkers on the subject presented at a conference in 1999 that addressed the fundamental question on the importance of culture in economic development. Co-edited with Samuel Huntington, this volume was published as *Culture Matters* in 2000.

The response to this volume was far greater than expected and led to the Culture Matters Research Project, consisting of 65 scholars. Fifty-one research papers were presented at two conferences in 2003 and 2004 and were published in two volumes of case studies.[1,2] In 2006 Harrison distilled the findings into the book, *The Central Liberal Truth*, and addressed the natural follow on question to *Culture Matters*: Can culture be shaped and, if so, how? The title comes from Senator Daniel Moynihan:

> The central conservative truth is that it is culture, not politics that determines the success of a society. The central liberal truth is that politics can change a culture and save it from itself.

In 2013, Harrison published his crowning achievement, *Jews, Confucians, and Protestants: Cultural Capital and the End of Multiculturalism*. This volume explores the cultural drivers of prosperity and freedom and presents a 25 trait typology of "universal progress culture," which

---

1   Harrison, Lawrence and Kagan, Jerome eds. (2006) *Developing Cultures: Essays in Cultural Change*, Rutledge.

2   Harrison, Lawrence and Berger, Peter eds. (2006) *Developing Cultures: Case Studies*, Rutledge.

is based on the original essay by Mariana Grondona in *Culture Matters* and then modified by four others; Iraki Chkonia, Lawrence Harrison, Matteo Marini, and Ronald Inglehart. This is summarized in the following table:

Typology of High Cultural Capital and Low Cultural Capital Societies

Based on the original structure of Mariano Grondona with inputs from Irakli Chkonia, Lawrence Harrison, Matteo Marini, and Ronald Inglehart.

Factor	High Cultural Capital	Low Cultural Capital
WORLDVIEW		
1. Religion	Nurtures rationality, achievement; promotes material pursuits; focus on this world; pragmatism	Nurtures irrationality; inhibits material pursuits; focus on the other world; utopianism
2. Destiny	I can influence my destiny for the better.	Fatalism, resignation, sorcery
3. Time Orientation	Future focus promotes planning, punctuality, deferred gratification	Present or past focus discourages planning, punctuality, saving
4. Wealth	Product of human creativity, expandable (positive sum)	What exists (zero-sum)
5. Knowledge	Practical, verifiable; facts matter	Abstract, theoretical, cosmological, not verifiable; debate matters
VALUES, VIRTUES		
6. Ethical code	Rigorous within realistic norms; feeds trust	Elastic, wide gap between utopian norms and behavior; mistrust
7. The Lesser Virtues	A job well done, tidiness, courtesy, punctuality matters	Lesser virtues unimportant; love, justice, courage matter
8. Education	Indispensable; promotes autonomy, heterodoxy, dissent, creativity	Less priority; promotes dependency, orthodoxy

Typology of High Cultural Capital and Low Cultural Capital Societies

Based on the original structure of Mariano Grondona with inputs from Irakli Chkonia, Lawrence Harrison, Matteo Marini, and Ronald Inglehart.

Factor	High Cultural Capital	Low Cultural Capital
ECONOMIC BEHAVIOR		
9. Work / Achievement	Live to work: work leads to wealth	Work to live: work doesn't lead to wealth; work is for the poor
10. Frugality	The mother of investment and property	A threat to equality
11. Entrepreunership	Investment and creativity	Rent-seeking
12. Risk Propensity	Moderate	Low; occasional adventures
13. Competition	Leads to excellence	Aggression; a threat to equality and privilege
14. Innovation	Open; rapid adaptation	Suspicious; slow adaptation
15. Advancement	Merit, achievement	Family, patron, connections
SOCIAL BEHAVIOR		
16. Rule of Law	Reasonably law abiding; corruption is prosecuted	Money, connections matter; corruption is tolerated
17. Radius of Identification and Trust	Stronger identification with the broader society	Stronger identification with the narrow community
18. Family	The idea of "family" extends to the broader society	The family is a fortress against the broader society
19. Association (social capital)	Trust, identification breed cooperation affiliation, participation	Mistrust breeds excessive individualism, anomie
20. The Individual/the Group	Emphasizes the individual but not excessively	Emphasizes the collectivity

Typology of High Cultural Capital and Low Cultural Capital Societies		
Based on the original structure of Mariano Grondona with inputs from Irakli Chkonia, Lawrence Harrison, Matteo Marini, and Ronald Inglehart.		
Factor	*High Cultural Capital*	*Low Cultural Capital*
21. Authority	Dispersed: checks and balances, consensus	Centralized: unfettered, often arbitrary
22. Role of Elites	Responsibility to society	Power and rent seeking; exploitative
23. Church / State Relationship	Secularized; wall between church and state	Religion plays major role in civic sphere
24. Gender Relationships	If not a reality, equality at least not inconsistent with value system; should also apply to gender preference	Women subordinated to men in most dimensions of life; gays/lesbians are discriminated against
25. Fertility	The number of children depends on the family's capacity to raise and educate them	Children are the gifts of God; they are an economic asset
Source: Lawrence Harrison (2013), *Jews, Christians, and Protestants*, Crown. Reproduced with permission.		

While biography is not destiny, it is worth recapping Harrison's professional background, as it shaped his work. From 1962 to 1982, Harrison was an official of the United States Agency for International Development and directed missions in five Latin American countries. In his words:

"What also became increasingly apparent to me was a pattern of problems that were common, in greater or lesser degree, to all the countries in which I worked, among them disrespect for the law, unbridled exercise of authority, lack of cooperation with one another, passivity when encountering problems, lack of civic consciousness, lack of trust, and pursuit of narrow personal interest. To be sure, these shortcomings are in all human societies, including the United States. But the degree of intensity of all the problems in Latin America seemed to me to be much greater. And the problems were clearly linked to Latin America's difficulties in consolidating democracy and social justice, and producing prosperity for its people. The array of fundamental problems was, I believed, deeply rooted in the minds of Latin Americans."[3]

In 1982, he retired from the Foreign Service to study these ideas in a scholarly setting. Samuel Huntington, at Harvard, invited Harrison to join the Center for International Affairs. At Harvard and then at the Fletcher School at Tufts, Harrison led the research on culture and founded the Cultural Change Institute, which is now in transition from the Fletcher School to the Hoover Institution at Stanford.

Our paths crossed in 2009 when I used the original Grondona framework published in Culture Matters to analyze General Motors and wrote, "Retooling GM's Culture" (see Appendix III). The typology was a powerful lens for understanding GM's culture, much richer than any I had read in the business literature. I sent Harrison the paper as a courtesy and to my surprise he reached out and we began a serious conversation about the role of culture in corporations. He challenged me to answer the same fundamental questions he had: what is the definition of a "good" corporate culture and how can culture be changed?

Four logical questions helped us reach a workable definition of good culture.

1. Does culture matter in business?
2. What do we mean by "good?"
3. Does the Harrison model fit? If not, how must the model be modified?
4. Even if valid, is the theory *useful* to business leaders?

We do not feel compelled to answer the first question. It seems obvious, based on our experience and that of many others. If someone does not believe that culture matters at this point, no evidence would convince him or her otherwise. Business leaders do believe that culture is important, but are frustrated by the current knowledge state, which does not give enough depth to help them manage it effectively. So the problem is not whether culture matters, but how useful is our understanding?

Chapter One defined "good," but we recap here. "Good" corporate culture means *profitable*: the values leading to sustainable economic success in the marketplace. Please note this has nothing to do with

---

3   Harrison, Lawrence, (2008). *The Central Liberal Truth: How Politics Can Change a Culture and Save It from Itself,* The Oxford University Press.

values that we, as individuals, might find attractive. A culture of profitability is not always pleasant or congenial. Some people confuse "pleasant" with a lack of discipline, laziness, unwillingness to debate, and failing to hold people accountable, including firing them for poor performance.

The second question is whether Harrison's model is valid, even as a starting point. After all, the research explains the prosperity of nations, not companies. The case for the model seems strong. Prosperity in a nation means that the businesses within it are successful, as the criteria were freedom and economic success. So clearly, these values had to apply broadly to businesses within the society, as many empirical studies validate the model of culture. These findings would not apply to enterprises in either criminal or communist societies.

But there were clearly some ways the Universal Progress Culture needed to be modified to explain business success. In the body of the book, we discussed the need to make the conceptual distinction between cultural traits applying to core purpose, aligning the outside world with the specific business model of the company (the instrumental values), and the common cultural infrastructure. We will not repeat the arguments here, but we will talk about how we proceeded from the 25 cultural traits of the Universal Progress Culture to the 13 that define the common cultural infrastructure.

In making this translation, we drove for parsimony, clarity, and fit. One helpful and rigorous review took place at the Samuel Huntington Memorial Conference in Moscow in 2010. Here thirty scholars, including three Nobel prize winners, met over three days and provided the initial audience for our typology. It produced discussion and approval. After some more deliberation, presenting the results at two more conferences and testing them with three multi-nationals, we compressed them to the thirteen qualities that form the minimum basis for defining a universal profitable culture for business in capitalist and democratic societies. Undoubtedly they will be further refined over time.

The translation is given in the following table:

Harrison Typology	Culture of Profitability Attribute
23. Church-state Relations 25. Fertility	N/A
17. Radius of Identification 18. Family	1. External Focus
4. Wealth 19. Association (social capital) 20. The Individual/the Group	2. Internal Trust
13. Competition 15. Advancement 22. Role of Elites	3. Merit and Accountability
1. Religion 5. Knowledge	4. Debate, Dissent, and Discipline
2. Destiny	5. Empowered
21. Authority	6. Decisions Where They Belong
3. Time Orientation	7. Forward Looking
10. Frugality 11. Entrepreneurship 12. Risk Propensity	8. Frugality and Investment
14. Innovation	9. Innovation
7. The Lesser Virtues 9. Work / Achievement	10. Strong Work Ethic
6. Ethical Code 16. Rule of Law / Corruption	11. Ethics
8. Education	12. Continuous Learning
24. Gender Relationships	13. Ability Matters Most

The translation is straight forward, with a couple of exceptions:

♦ Attitude towards wealth is mapped into Internal Trust. High cultural capital countries view wealth as a positive sum and a product of creativity, therefore a big driver of trust and willingness to cooperate. If people in a company see the pie as limited, one person's gain is another's loss. Distrust will surely follow.

♦ Religion is mapped into Debate, Dissent, and Discipline. The characteristic of religion that maps into Debate, Dissent, and Discipline is the emphasis on rationality and pragmatism, as opposed to irrationality and utopianism. Knowledge and facts matter, and should be verifiable, and practical.

One of the tangential lessons from our work is the importance of cross-disciplinary studies. The business academics who study culture have been oblivious to the work of the development experts, and vice versa. The lack of communication has probably impeded both sides, but especially those tilling the fields of business.

To be of use, the theory must provide tools that let business diagnose and manage culture. The problem with the existing theories was their generality. Granularity and detail are necessary for a theory is to be applied. Otherwise it is all vague generalities.

The second criterion for usefulness is that the ideas must be straightforward enough for business leaders to understand and use themselves, just as they would any important business driver. That does not mean the thinking must be simplistic, but it must be neither brain surgery nor rocket science, nor must it depend on a long-standing army of expensive outsiders. The model we offer meets these criteria well. It is detailed enough to distinguish different areas of culture, and it has suitable diagnostics. The model is complex enough to describe reality but simple enough to be used.

We tested our model, as described in Chapter 15, given the availability of public data and came away reassured of the model's validity (enough to put our personal savings behind our words).

Appendix II:
Retooling GM's Culture

Originally Published February 16, 2009

Note: We include this article as a matter of historical interest. Writing this article had several consequences. It provided the "tipping point" on the consensus that culture was a major problem at General Motors. This seems deeply immodest but I believe it to be true. It was certainly not the first article to say GM's culture was a problem, but it was timed well. It came out just as the government was considering what do and while the old management team of Rick Wagoner's was still in place. Any intelligent outsider would have seen the culture was deeply flawed but the complexity and press of events made it difficult to understand precisely how, or the true depth of the problem. This article helped outsiders understand it more clearly, and have greater confidence in their judgment that radical steps were needed to save the company, beginning with changing the Board and management team but going much further.

The final outcome was Lawrence Harrison reaching out to me and encouraging me to take a deeper look at the role of culture in the private sector.

Even though several years have now passed, we believe that the article is still relevant, interesting, and worth reading, hence it is included here. (There are a few minor changes in wording and grammar from the original.)

GM has developed a plan for the US government that is supposed to demonstrate its long run viability. The company is looking at its products, brands, manufacturing footprint and capacity, health care, and "structural costs," while negotiating with the UAW to further reduce labor costs. All this is well and good but it is almost certain that GM is not addressing an issue that, in the long run, could be more important than all these others: its culture.

Mentioning the "C" word makes eyes roll, as it is seen as too "soft" to deal with in a meaningful way and does not matter anyway, once the "real" stuff has been taken care. But to a long run observer of the company, it is apparent that unless GM's culture is fundamentally changed, especially in North America, its true heart, GM will likely be back at the public trough again and again until the public finally grows weary and allows its demise. It is unlikely to achieve sustained profitability unless it fixes its culture and it may even be true that once the culture is fixed, the business will take care of itself.

Culture means the "values, attitudes, beliefs, and underlying assumptions."[1] The importance of culture is that it forms the foundation of the business logic brought to any specific decision or problem; there is little chance something will be done that violates the culture, as it would mean contradicting fundamental beliefs. The success of many companies, including McKinsey, P&G, and Pixar is attributed to their cultures and a recent study of Toyota concluded its success is due as much to its culture as the Toyota Production System.[2] Sometimes societies may change their culture in response to a major disruption, as Germany and Japan did after World War II and companies have as well, such as GE, IBM and Alberto-Culver,[3] after their own near-death experiences. But in all these cases there was a consensus among the leadership that the culture needed to change and serious efforts were put in place to implement those changes. It is fairly apparent from their behavior and statements that GM leadership in North America do not believe there is anything fundamentally wrong with the company's culture; indeed they seem firmly convinced that they were well on their way to recovery but were overtaken by events beyond their control; specifically the large spike in energy prices and the collapse of the credit markets that have led to the current recession.

GM's current response seems to reflect its fundamental beliefs about the way the world works and it is almost identical to what it has been doing for the last 30 years: cut "structural costs," wait for future products to bring salvation, and count on cash from the other regions

1   Harrison, Lawrence E. and Huntington, Samuel P. eds. (2000) *Culture Matters: How Values Shape Human Progress*, Basic Books. The 9 traits used in this article are derived from 10 given in Harrison's essay in the book, "Promoting Progressive Cultural Change" and the definition of culture comes from Huntington's Foreword.
2   Takeuchi, Hirotaka, Emi Osono, and Norihiko Shimizu (2008) "The Contradictions that Drive Toyota's Success," Harvard Business Review.
3   For the Alberto-Culver story, see Bernick, Carol Lavin (2001) "When Your Culture Needs a Makeover," Harvard Business Review.

(and, now, the government) to help prop things up in the meantime, but make no truly fundamental change in the business, its structure or people running it, as they are clearly the best and brightest, know how to manage things in a serious way, and have a sound plan. The proposed changes are touted as "profound" and "fundamental" but are really the minimum change from status quo the company believes it can get away with. There is a profound reluctance to make hard decisions that would cause short term pain but would lead to fixing the problem in the long run; instead there is a continual compromise of action that leads to too little too late but defers immediate catastrophe. This is reflected in every aspect of the enterprise, from decisions on manufacturing, which never brings capacity into line with market realities, to people, where almost no one is ever fired for poor performance. This has not worked yet and it is difficult to believe it will work now.

The scholars Lawrence Harrison, Samuel Huntington, and their colleagues have addressed the fundamental question of whether culture "matters" in how societies develop and make a compelling case that it matters a great deal. They have also outlined the specific traits that lead a society to progress or prevent it from doing so and their work provides a rigorous way to think about culture that is based on substantial evidence. These traits seem applicable to a private enterprise, especially one that is larger and older than many countries.

1. **Progressive cultures emphasize the future; static cultures emphasize the present or past.** GM, unfortunately, lives in its past glory, as there were always better times in days gone by. Like the UK before Thatcherism, there is a deep sense that their value is their heritage, not what they are going to do tomorrow. While there have been pockets that have looked forward, and serious investments in fuel cells, there is little belief that the future is theirs to make.

2. **Work is central to the good life in progressive cultures but a burden in static cultures.** This is a mixed story for GM as there is generally a very strong work ethic, but it is confined to the elites more than the rank and file, whether union or company. For the white and blue collar workers, there is much more emphasis on leisure and "the good life" than the value of hard work. So you will find certain groups working 70 hour weeks routinely but others who will get angry if you even suggest working over a weekend or a vacation. And somewhat perversely, the groups that

do work very long hours are driven to it by a few leaders who think that is a constant requirement, with the consequence that work becomes inefficient and fills the required time, rather than being driven by sensible needs to do whatever it takes to win.

3. **Frugality and investment are valued in progressive societies but seen as a threat in static cultures.** GM seems to have redefined the notion of investment as cost cutting. For some reason, time after time, the company believes it can reduce its capital investment in products whenever times get bad without having to pay for it in consequences of compromised characteristics and lower share and price. The company also seems willing to save $1 in capital even if it costs $100 in incentives. For a company run by finance people, they seem to have lost all notion of what investment means, in product or people. Further, when they have made investments that were different and quite successful, such as NUMMI, Saturn, and then later OnStar and Hummer, they were made reluctantly and never really embraced by the organization, but seen as threats or outsiders. GMDAT, its Korean joint venture, has been a tremendous and unanticipated success, but is viewed with condescension and even deeply resented by many.

4. **Education is critically important to progressive cultures, but only marginally important in static ones, except to elites.** GM is squarely in the static camp. It talks about all the training it does, but in fact it is almost all peripheral; GM University, which was launched with soaring rhetoric, is of little to no importance, unlike Crottonville for GE. Sure, the managers all have MBAs and the standard path is still an undergraduate engineering degree from GMI and a Harvard MBA, but there is little emphasis placed on ongoing education and most of the programs that were in existence were among the first casualties of "structural cost reductions."

5. **In progressive societies, merit is central to advancement but in static ones it is family and connections.** On this point, GM probably gets mixed to negative reviews. The sense is that one must be part of the club to advance, which usually means the right degree from the right school, the right path, and knowing the top guys,

who are your mentors. Twenty years ago, GM would have been completely in the static dimension on this attribute, but there has been substantial progress in reaching out to groups that had been excluded in the past and advancing them on their merits. Unfortunately, this has been much truer for GM's operations outside of North America and Western Europe than for these two core regions. In North America, the tradition is to pick high IQ people with the right background at an early age and then to rotate them through a series of "developmental" assignments. The consequence is that the people who rise to the very top are very smart with broad experience, but they are almost never people who have truly accomplished anything; who have never built something from scratch or grown a business from small to large or turned around a losing operation into a profitable one.

6. **In progressive cultures, people identify with groups well beyond the family and into society.** GM falls directly into the static side. Despite substantial effort to create "one company," GM is still surprisingly full of provincialism, based on both function and geography. Very few GM employees see themselves as truly belonging to the global enterprise; almost all identify themselves with their function and then the local business unit, viewing others as ignorant meddlers and sometimes outright adversaries. While many companies have embraced the notion of the "extended enterprise" and successfully manage complex alliance relationships, GM's investments in major alliances (Fuji, Suzuki, Isuzu, and Fiat) were all great disappointments and had little if any return.

Of all GM's cultural problems, this might be the most crippling as it perpetuates an inward focus that is largely responsible for its hostile relations with its dealers and suppliers and, most troubling, with consumers. As a consequence of its insularity, the company has repeatedly displayed behavior that shows it to be tone deaf to society and much of the external world has written off the company.

7. **Ethical codes are more important in progressive cultures. Here GM gets high marks.** There have been few corruption scandals, sexual harassment is not permitted,

there is strict adherence to the Foreign Corrupt Practices Act, and the company will not let itself be associated with "shady" characters or businesses. While any company of its size and scope will have incidents, the ethical codes at GM are high and enforced.

8. **Authority tends to be horizontal and decentralized in progressive cultures and centralized and vertical in static cultures.** Authority at GM is centralized and probably becoming more so as the company "globalizes" by creating strong, centrally controlled global functions that further weaken regional autonomy. While there are regional and functional strategy boards that have the appearance of dispersing authority, in fact they are all controlled by the same few people. One of the perverse outcomes of globalizing functions is that authority is becoming "horizontal" and strongly centralized, as global functions that are all run from Detroit become the main lines of authority and undercut the business units.

9. **Progressive cultures are secular, with limited influence of religious culture and a high degree of tolerance of heterodoxy and dissent.** GM scores fairly low on this attribute. There is little tolerance of strong dissent from the prevailing opinion, although there is substantial subversion and passive-aggressive resistance. In discussions about setting direction, much more attention is given to wondering what the senior leadership will think than to figuring out the right path and trying to make it happen. The very senior people are often spoken of in tones of reverence and are seldom debated in any meaningful way.

Altogether, this is a fairly depressing picture. GM has been explicit about its cultural priorities: "One Company, Stretch, Sense of Urgency, and Product and Customer Focus," but there has been little attention to making these real beyond reiterating them at quarterly meetings.

What is fascinating about GM, and offers some hope, is that it really has two cultures. The one described above is an accurate depiction of the culture in North America and Western Europe, but there is another in the rest of the world that is very different. The culture of GM's operations in Asia, Latin America, Africa and Middle East, Russia and Eastern Europe, is much more progressive and it is in these areas that GM is doing very well. On almost all of the measures listed above, they would come out on the progressive side. Working for GM in Asia Pacific, Latin America, or the Middle East, you would think you were in a completely different company. People are very forward looking, they are capable of making the tough decisions, they are business focused, debate is tolerated but discipline is enforced, relations with their labor force and dealers are usually positive, and authority is genuinely dispersed to the smaller business units within each of the regions.

Numerous people have commented on the difference in economic health and attributed it to the absence of the UAW, retiree's health care burden, and government regulations such as CAFE. While these are important, it is misleading to attribute the differences to these factors. Since many of these issues are the result of the deliberate policy choices of GM, they are more symptoms of the underlying malaise than the cause; plus the healthy regions all have tremendous challenges of their own that are not present in North America or Western Europe, where the static culture is really confined.

Many of the people running GM have had extensive international experience. There is a common practice of rotating executives on the CEO track to international postings; the classic path for a high potential finance executive from a traditional background is to be made head of GM Brazil; a business unit whose culture is quite progressive and has been consistently profitable over many years. Rather peculiarly, there is very little rotation of executives who have "grown up" in overseas operations into the key spots in North America. With a couple of exceptions, none of the top team has spent the majority of their careers in these regions that have been the most successful. Furthermore, Asia Pacific and Latin America/Africa/Middle East are headed up by people with quite different backgrounds. One is British, the other is a female Canadian lawyer; neither have spent the majority of their careers in Detroit. The people operating the lower level business units in these healthy regions tend to be either foreign born or Americans who are considered "different" and who have quite deliberately chosen to stay as far from Detroit as possible, often explicitly to avoid a culture they find stultifying and dismaying. Despite the progressive nature of the culture overseas and its consistent success, there seems little propensity to bring these people back into North America or Western Europe; somehow they are simply never seen as "developed" enough. When one or two promising individuals are brought back, they are often overwhelmed by the dominant culture in Detroit and either head back overseas quickly, leave the company, or fade into obscurity.

Twenty years ago, Elmer Johnson, a successful outside lawyer recruited into GM's top ranks and a candidate for CEO, wrote a memo to the senior leadership, recently posted in Barron's,[4] which was heartbreakingly prophetic. Its central theme was that GM's culture was preventing it from executing its strategy and unless there was a concerted effort to change its culture, there would be little chance of meaningful change. He was ignored and shortly afterwards left the company. His prophecy that GM would fail in its bid to become a company that built the world's best cars and trucks in a way that provided superior shareholder value has, regrettably, proven disastrously true. The recommendations he made – major changes in people at the top, the committee structures, the organizational structure, and decision making process – are still sound but now would not go nearly far enough.

This raises the question of what can be done. The first and most obvious is to change a significant number of people at the very top, replacing them either with outsiders or with GM executives from overseas operations who have not grown up in the traditional culture. While there is much attention on the CEO, his removal is hardly sufficient and, if done as an isolated sacrifice, would simply perpetuate the status quo. The change in management should go several levels down but also include substantial changes in the Board of Directors, as they are key enablers and drivers of the corporate culture. The Board has not put any pressure on management to change its culture or drive accountability; on the contrary they have consistently re-stated their support of the management team. There are few if any real change agents on GM's Board. Changing large numbers of people at the top is a necessary but not sufficient condition, as the static culture is reinforced by so many other attributes.

Serious consideration needs to be given to a radically different organization that would give people overall business responsibility and accountability and increase their contact with markets and the external world. The current direction is to move away from integrated business responsibility by creating strong functions with weak business units, and making the transition slowly compounds the problem, so there is continual confusion and conflict over who is responsible for what. The company is doing this to "leverage its global strengths" but the real effect is to create an organization where fewer and fewer people are actually running a business or have contact with the outside world and control is becoming more and more concentrated in a few people.

---

4   http://s.wsj.net/public/resources/documents/BA_gm_memo.pdf . This is definitely worth a read.

Education and training need to be made part of everyone's life, from the most junior to the most senior. This becomes even more important in times of stress, as it demonstrates long term commitment to people and, more importantly, to the future. A portion of this education should take place outside of GM to increase exposure to people outside the industry. In the scheme of things, the costs of education and training are truly negligible. If someone asks to calculate the ROI, it should be used as a litmus test for determining candidates for structural cost reductions.

GM's decision-making processes need serious revamping. Despite improvements, most meetings are still exercises in procrastination, rubber stamping or idea killing, without anything that would pass for genuine debate and dialogue. Dealing with complex issues requires genuine discussion, feedback, and intellectual engagement. Changing the people, along with the structure, should help enable this key cultural change but there must also be a conscious choice among the leadership that they want to make this transformation.

These modifications would also disrupt patronage relationships and should permit merit to become more important, especially if there is an influx of outsiders and overseas managers. Also, in the same way that having an African American become president of the United States will change many American's notion of what it means to be an American and what can be accomplished, having someone who is genuinely "different" will help many people in the company see GM differently. If the competent people in Brazil see that there is a real chance they can reach the top, it will change their level of engagement and the company will be much better for it.

Implementing these changes piecemeal will not be enough to make meaningful changes in GM's culture because they are all necessary to reinforce one another to grow a different and progressive culture that is self-sustaining. The more challenging question is whether the people currently running the enterprise would ever implement them in the climate of crisis. They are certainly intellectually capable of doing so, but seem wedded to the momentum plan and believe that their main task is to get through the current crisis and to re-negotiate its labor contracts, trim its dealer body and brand portfolio, and lower its cost structure, not deal with cultural drivers. The mainstay belief is that all will turn out well if only they have the chance to implement their plans, starting with the much-heralded Volt. Then they will consider turning their attention to considering these types of "secondary" issues.

What you believe about this position depends on your level of confidence in the company's ability to execute its plans, which have always sounded good and well-reasoned. These operational issues are absolutely critical to the future of GM. The importance of dealing with the culture is that unless there is a substantial change in the company's beliefs and values, the most likely outcome is that, once again, too little will be done too late. The very real crisis the company is in would permit GM to make the cultural changes that would be very difficult in "normal" times and provide a once-in-a-generation opportunity to transform GM back into a global powerhouse. GM has so many talented people in it and almost certainly has the potential to turn around, but not until it develops a culture that lets it be truly progressive rather than one that continually defers the hard choices, holds it back, stops talented people from making contributions, and prevents its plans from becoming reality.

Post Script I: Bio and Motivation

I have been a consultant for GM for 15 years and an employee for 9 years prior to that, and have worked at one time or another in almost every region and function. This paper has not been endorsed or supported in any way by anyone at GM; I suspect it will be harshly rejected (or simply ignored) at the senior levels but will strike a deep chord a few levels down. This is written out of the deepest affection for the company and it is an attempt to deal with a fundamental issue that has kept the company from success and is now critical to its long term viability. The people who do care about GM, and there are many, and who think a future is still possible need to stand up and try to make a difference, regardless of the short run costs.

Appendix III:
Why Did Such a Nice Guy Finish Last?

This essay was written in June 2009 and is reproduced here with only minor changes. It is included as an appendix because it elaborates on one of the more insidious forces of cultural entropy: niceness.

Most people who met Rick Wagoner walked away with the feeling that here was a real nice guy. He was not a pompous "suit," he did not have a big entourage, he was never abusive to subordinates; he was amiable, bright, and engaging. Yet his tenure as a CEO saw the company's descent to ruin. Like Rick, most of the past CEO's were pretty decent guys but also saw GM decline on their watch. In fact, most of the management team are very nice people.

Niceness is part of GM's culture and is driven by several causes. Most leaders have been insiders recruited at an early age, told that they were headed for the top and could expect to work with the same set of people for most of their careers. They had short stints in their specific assignments, which meant they never saw the long run consequences of their actions. But they were hurt if there was a short run problem, so conflict was avoided and problems were swept away and passed over to the next guy to deal with. Mix this with broad insularity from the market place, complete faith that GM would always be there, and a very hierarchical organization that places the boss on a pedestal.

This all meant that relationships were more important than anything else, especially within the "ruling class." The hierarchical nature of the organization, where people take their cues from their superiors, ensured a widespread culture of affability. It is noteworthy that the only ones who really contradicted this mold were outsiders brought in at the top level or people whose careers at GM were overseas, which has a very different corporate culture.

This issue deserves attention as GM decides what kind of culture it wants after emerging from Chapter 11. Did all this niceness contribute to the disaster or was it just an artifact of GM's culture and midwest location? The dictionary defines nice as: pleasing, amiable, agreeable, kind, pleasant. What is wrong with that? In GM's case, quite a bit.

The niceness stood in the way of figuring out what to do. Hard problems require real debate; they are not solved by the smartest guy (or the CEO) going off to a dark room and coming back with the answer. Lively arguments sharpen thinking, get people out of their comfort zone, raise the important issues, and lead to creative solutions. They also ensure that everyone at least feels their points were heard and given proper consideration, which helps a great deal in implementing whatever decision is taken. When people are too nice, serious discussion does not take place, they get to a "consensus" but not the best answer. False smiles lead to passive-aggressive resistance, political posturing, and focusing on what the boss wants rather than figuring out the best decision. It undermines anything being done at all. Or people follow their boss off the cliff because no one was able to warn him away.

Part of GM's legacy is fear of anti-trust action. As the biggest elephant, it was unafraid of the tigers walking around and even had to make sure not to harm them for fear of the trust busters. This was two generations ago, but it has persisted in GM's culture. Leadership views other auto companies somewhere between allies and competitors in a tough basketball game, rather than enemies. While there are some real areas of cooperation, including joint ventures, regulatory issues and shared suppliers, there has never been a willingness to try to figure out how to really beat the other guys. But the world is now a viciously competitive place. It is certain that GM's competitors from Asia want to win the market completely, they could not care less about being nice guys, and there is nothing wrong with that. The only reason these competitors have not tried to kill GM is their fear of political consequences. But it is certain that those fears are diminishing as the public loses it affection for the Detroit Three. GM has played under Marquess of Queensberry rules where it has been, and will be, in a knife fight that plays out over a long period of time.

Running a successful business means keeping order in your own house. Every member of the team wants to help but also wants the biggest slice of the pie. Everyone has a natural tendency to think their contribution is the source of all good things and deserve to be rewarded accordingly. They all need to be told "no," repeatedly, and firm boundaries need to be drawn or there will always be conflict over the pie. GM's niceness has led to some bad behavior by everyone, as no one seems to have ever been willing to really say no and crack the whip. Ironically, the result is mutual distrust and hostility, as everyone feels shafted by the others, but are, of course, too nice to really say so (at least to each other's face). To emerge from Chapter 11, GM is going to inflict even more pain than it has so far; everyone will hurt. But being nice and not doing what really needs to be done would mean the true end of GM.

In the business world, it is important to be effective. Carlos Ghosn, the world's most respected automotive CEO, is not a mean man, but no one talks about what a nice guy he is either; likewise Sergio Marchionne at Fiat. When people talk of Bill Gates, it is not about what a nice guy he is. Alfred Sloan, the founder of GM and the 20th century's greatest business genius, was a gentleman but not famous for being a nice man. Henry Ford was at best eccentric and at worst anti-Semitic and bigoted. But all these men were effective.

Giving bad news and debating the difficult issues, fighting hard and doing everything to win, setting boundaries and enforcing discipline and accountability – these are the building blocks of a winning culture. Mutual respect, collegiality, good manners, and having a little fun are important to make it all work, and make the world a better place, but let's forget about being nice.

Index

About the Authors
Rob Kleinbaum

Rob Kleinbaum, founder of RAK & Co, has over 30 years of experience working in industry and consulting. He has worked on a wide variety of projects in many industries and countries. A common theme is problems rooted in multiple issues and culture. His wife and partner, Aviva, has always understood the importance of culture and their debates, along with his experience, started them on the road that led to *Creating A Culture of Profitability*.

Quoted extensively in the global press, Dr. Kleinbaum has been featured on NPR, MSNBC, BBC, the LA Times, Reuters, Asahi Shimbun, and has been quoted by David Brooks in the New York Times. He is on the Executive Committee of the Cultural Change Institute and is a Fellow and former Board member of the Society of Decision Professionals.

Dr. Kleinbaum was also a partner at Strategic Decisions Group, a major global consulting company, and an executive and founder of General Motors' Decision Support Center, a leading internal consulting company. He received a PhD in Economics from the University of Michigan at Ann Arbor, where he was also a Research Scientist and Visiting Assistant Professor of Economics. Rob also has a BA in Sociology from the University of Michigan.

About the Authors
Aviva Kleinbaum

Aviva Kleinbaum, a Director at RAK & Co, has 15 years of experience in consulting and leadership coaching. Her work focuses in executive coaching and creating cultural and organization changes that drive major business improvements. Ms. Kleinbaum helps people develop the abilities they need to become successful leaders and valued team members. Aviva's clients have been in the fields of law, marketing, services, and manufacturing, in the United States and internationally.

Aviva has been personal coach to several human resources vice presidents, working on interpersonal relations, cultural diversity, conflict management, and on integrating corporate culture into new strategic directions.

Ms. Kleinbaum is a psychotherapist by training. Aviva has been Director of Clinical Programs for two psycho-therapy clinics and was in private practice for many years. She holds a Bachelor and Master of Social Work degrees from University of Michigan in Ann Arbor and is a Certified Clinical Psychotherapist. She is speaks three languages and has been a public lecturer on change and culture. Aviva was an Adviser to the Israeli Parliament Subcommittee on Defusing Cultural Differences. She is also an accomplished artist, working in several forms, and her art can be seen at www.avivanadia.com.